SpringerBriefs in Sociology

AF848754

More information about this series at http://www.springer.com/series/10410

Vitor Eduardo Schincariol

Society and Economy in Venezuela

An Overview of the Bolivarian Period (1998-2018)

Springer

Vitor Eduardo Schincariol
Federal University of ABC
Santo André, São Paulo, Brazil

ISSN 2212-6368 ISSN 2212-6376 (electronic)
SpringerBriefs in Sociology
ISBN 978-3-030-60082-2 ISBN 978-3-030-60083-9 (eBook)
https://doi.org/10.1007/978-3-030-60083-9

© The Editor(s) (if applicable) and The Author(s), under exclusive license to Springer Nature Switzerland AG 2020
This work is subject to copyright. All rights are reserved by the Publisher, whether the whole or part of the material is concerned, specifically the rights of translation, reprinting, reuse of illustrations, recitation, broadcasting, reproduction on microfilms or in any other physical way, and transmission or information storage and retrieval, electronic adaptation, computer software, or by similar or dissimilar methodology now known or hereafter developed.
The use of general descriptive names, registered names, trademarks, service marks, etc. in this publication does not imply, even in the absence of a specific statement, that such names are exempt from the relevant protective laws and regulations and therefore free for general use.
The publisher, the authors, and the editors are safe to assume that the advice and information in this book are believed to be true and accurate at the date of publication. Neither the publisher nor the authors or the editors give a warranty, expressed or implied, with respect to the material contained herein or for any errors or omissions that may have been made. The publisher remains neutral with regard to jurisdictional claims in published maps and institutional affiliations.

This Springer imprint is published by the registered company Springer Nature Switzerland AG
The registered company address is: Gewerbestrasse 11, 6330 Cham, Switzerland

Preface

Hugo Chávez's administrations in Venezuela (1998–2013) represented great political and social changes for this nation. Assuming power under a developmentalist and then socialist perspective, Chávez's administrations introduced new positive political and social features in Venezuela. After an unstable period between 1998–2002, Venezuela also achieved high rates of economic growth until 2007; however, growth dropped after 2008, and with the exception of the 2009–2012 interlude, the economy saw a constant decline. This decline was severely intensified after 2013, during the first presidency of Nicolás Maduro (2013–2018). According to the Economic Commission for Latin

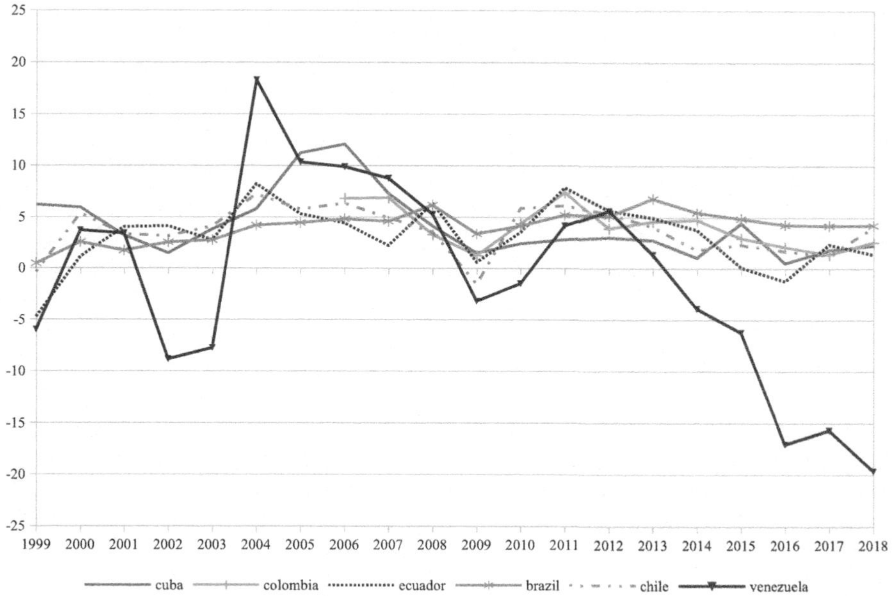

Latin America. Selected nations. Changes in GDP (%). 1999–2018. Constant domestic currencies. (Source: Cepal-Stat)

America and the Caribbean (ECLAC), from 2014 to 2017 the GDP fell by 40%, a recession never seen in the Venezuelan recent past (see Figure 1). Foreign reserves dropped to low levels (less than US$10 billion by 2018; see Figure 2) and consumer prices soared, reaching 180% in 2015, 826% in 2017, the government then losing control over prices. President Nicolás Maduro, however, was reelected in 2018.

In fact, all Latin American nations suffered declining rates of economic growth over the same period, but the dimension of the Venezuelan recession and its rates of inflation since 2018 had no parallel in the region. State's domestic and external debts raised and emigration soared. [1] In this sense, the dimension of this groundbreaking crisis and the particular political conditions prevailing in the nation—government's self-declared search for socialism amidst an ongoing economic prevalence of domestic private enterprises and in a world dominated by neoliberal globalization—constitute enough reasons for analyzing Venezuela's overall socioeconomic performance since 1998. In light of that, this work focuses on two questions: (1) Why did the Venezuelan economy show declining rates of growth from 2006 onwards? (2) Why did the economic crisis during the first Maduro administration become so severe? The study departs from the approach of the economic history, which mixes economic and social variables for the explanation of this type of research problem.

Venezuela. Foreign reserves. 1997–2018. Millions of US dollars. (Source: Central Bank of Venezuela ('Movimiento cambiario. Ingresos y egressos de divisas del Banco Central de Venezuela. Reservas Internacionales'))

[1] According to the United Nations Population Division, the inflow of Venezuelan emigrants remittances reached only US$ 17 million in 2000 and US$ 247 million by 2019. See United Nations (2019), International Migration Stock 2019 - Wall Chart. New York, United Nations Population Division. Available on: https://www.un.org/en/development/desa/population/migration/publications/wallchart/docs/MigrationStock2019_Wallchart.pdf

The recent history of Venezuela has attracted much attention, but still there are few broad and aggregate empirical accounts of the whole so-called Bolivarian Period that goes from 1999 to 2018 (the end of Maduro's first presidential term); these works often oscillate between ferocious critiques, uncritical assessments, or many advanced and independent case studies, particularly regarding political conditions, land reform, labor relations, and forms of ownership. This work runs the risks of analyzing in empirical terms the Venezuelan economic and social histories during the whole 1998–2018 interlude. The goal is to contribute to a broader account of the Bolivarian Period inaugurated in 1998, which includes all Hugo Chávez's presidential administrations as well as the first presidential term of Nicolás Maduro (1999–2013 and 2013–2018, respectively). Economic history is here taken in its broader sense, that is, in the multiple interrelations between economy and society. The ideas of Hugo Chávez and his political movement are taken seriously, although not under a sectarian stance.

This book is organized as follows. It departs from a brief summary of the Venezuelan historical background over the last century. Chapter 2 makes some considerations regarding the recent history of socialism and particularly of the economics of socialist planning; it then tackles the emergence of the leftist ideas in Venezuela at the end of the last century, focusing on Hugo Chávez's thoughts on these issues and interpreting them in light of the former discussion. Here, as well as for the other chapters, an eventual interest for the reader relies on the fact that we take Chávez's ideas on socialism and their consequences in terms of the adopted policies in Venezuela not only in light of their own but instead also from the point of view of the economics of socialist planning. A summary of the economic policies between Chavez's first election and the end of Maduro's first term as a president (2018) is followed in Chap. 3; the adopted policies are described in a chronological fashion and placed in their historical and economic context, the official documents that described the government's intentions being also described and analyzed. In Chap. 4, the work then turns to the empirical study of the macroeconomic performance of Venezuela over the 1999-2018 interlude. The empirical evaluation begins with the difference between the oil-sector and the non-oil sector, and then turns to the main macroeconomic aggregates and their corresponding expression in terms of the sectoral allocation; this section is concluded with a brief analysis of the employment structure. An analysis of the external sector of the economy is followed, beginning with Venezuela's foreign trade and then turning to aspects of the balance of payments as a whole. The last part of the empirical analysis focuses on fiscal and monetary aspects of the public policies, particularly in order to clarify why inflation rates became so high after 2013. The empirical analysis is followed by a final chapter with a summary of the empirical findings and some brief reflections.

A summary of our historical account, developed in the next chapters, goes as follows. Since the beginning of the present century, the Venezuelan economy saw a new boom in oil exports and this boom coincided with the new administration of Hugo Chávez, who firstly pursued developmentalist goals and then socialist ones after the coup attempt he suffered in 2002. Through the (re-)nationalization of PDVSA (*Petróleos de Venezuela*), the main oil enterprise in the nation, the government used the booming oil resources for different types of subsidies, domestic investments, and social expenditures, including an over-valuated exchange rate regime for imports of food and other tangible goods. Despite the many developmentalist and social policies introduced since 1999, the domestic economy followed the rise and then the fall in oil exports particularly between 2003–2008, GDP showing cumulative increases, though at declining rates, driven by swings in oil exports.

Chávez's first mix of several "heterodox" perspectives on economic and social development rightly assumed that a higher diversification of the economy was as an obvious necessity towards a lower dependence of the external cycles associated with oil exports. The government tried to implement this diversification through public investments, nationalizations, and subsidies. Empirical analysis shows that there was in fact a drop in the oil sector's contribution to GDP over time, the non-oil sectors of the economy growing faster over the period 1999–2008. There was indeed a higher degree of diversification of the domestic economy since then, which was translated into the growth of many types of new services and infrastructure, mainly focused on the internal, though "non-productive," sectors of the economy. [2] The nationalization of PDVSA represented a major shift in economic policies towards a higher control of the economy and national autonomy, in line with the perspectives that guided Chávez and his followers. The social polices undertaken by the administrations also fostered an improvement of social conditions, which could be verified in the form of the many available indicators, particularly housing and education conditions.

However, this relative diversification of the domestic economy was not translated into a higher manufacturing production and exporting capacities; the rate of imports to the GDP was rapidly raised after 2003, and manufacturing sectors dropped in relative terms. There was land distribution, the rising of cultivated areas, and other incentives to repeasantization, but agriculture also fell behind in relative terms, in parallel with growing urbanization. "Non-productive" services enjoyed higher rates of growth and employment. Despite their importance regarding the general improvement of social and economic conditions and eventually economies of scale, the type of economic growth since 1998 did not show "structural" changes and the economy still relied mainly on the surplus generated by oil exports by 2008, services adding not much in material terms. This performance can be largely, although not exclusively, explained by the overvalued exchange rate regimes which were adopted since 2004. Accordingly, the overall rate of investment (gross capital formation in terms of the GDP), with the exclusion of the 2003–2007 period, did not grow significantly. Beyond the fluctuations in oil markets, the economic policies did not lead to structural changes that prevented the high impacts of a new international crisis in 2008. In short, the government professed socialism after 2003, meaning self-management, land reform, and progressive social and economic measures, but also

[2] "Non-productive" here means the supply of intangible goods which cannot provide for a *material* surplus, that is, a physical difference between aggregate production and aggregate consumption, in line with the approach that goes from Paul Baran to Joan Robinson and Celso Furtado (see Baran 1957, Robinson 1979 and Furtado 2008).

the acceptance of a large private sector in the economy; therefore, the government did not implement an overall planning and the imposition of physical targets, that is, forced accumulation of capital, on an extensive scale. [3]

The year 2008 represented a major turning point in the economic conditions, because of the impacts of the international financial crisis on the oil markets. The oil sector was badly affected and never recovered, and this affected the economy as a whole. The following decade (2008–2018) saw multiple crises for the Venezuelan oil sector: declining oil prices, less imports of the Venezuelan oil by the United States (still the main trade partner), and then the economic sanctions applied by this nation since 2014, with particularly important economic sanctions since 2017 (see Chap. 4). Thus, there was an interruption of the previous type of growth based on oil exports and their reinvestments in the domestic economy. Falling oil exports gradually led to lower direct and indirect multiplier effects coming from the oil resources, particularly government investments and subsidies, as well as limits to import. As a mix of falling exports and sanctions, there was a fiscal and external crisis, leading to high inflation; beyond this cause, inflation had also other multiple roots (such as speculation), as we will see.

After 2008, the decline in the GDP growth rates continued to be linked to the external sector of the economy, but to this primary cause, others were added: the government did not alter the course of its above-mentioned economic policies, particularly regarding the exchange rate regime; and given the worsening living conditions, coupled with Chávez's death, social conflict and dissatisfaction with the government intensified. This led to broader political and economic opposition, particularly capital flights, economic terrorism, speculation, and hoarding. These factors, together with the ongoing fiscal crisis, lower foreign reserves, and expansionary monetary policies, led to hyperinflation during Maduro's first presidential term. Emigration rates soared.

The degree of involution of the economic parameters over these years has no parallel in the Venezuelan and maybe in the Latin American recent economic history. This is why it is important to try to grasp what happened in Venezuela over the last years. Of course, it is up to the Venezuelans to reflect upon the differences between the alternative models of economic policies, but this question is also of interest for the rest of Latin America and other so-called developing nations which still find in socialism relevant tools for political and economic mobilization. This is why this book may have a wider interest.

***

Some methodological comments should be made. The work draws on the available official documents of the Venezuelan government, and the available statistical data as furnished by the Central Bank of Venezuela, the Economic Commission for

[3] "Extensive growth in its pure form is based on quantitative increases in labour, capital and land, whereas intensive growth is derived from gains in overall productivity, i.e. increasing efficiency of labour and a better utilization of capital and other means of production" (Wilczynski 1972, p.25).

Latin America and the Caribbean, the International Energy Agency, and other official sources. All statistic data was accessed between May 2019 and July 2020.

When using and translating the data directly collected on the website of the Central Bank of Venezuela or another Venezuelan official source, I always mention its original expression in Spanish, as well as its original reference number such as informed by the corresponding website. Regarding the ECLAC statistical database—Cepal-Stat—the majority of its primary data relies ultimately on the Central Bank of Venezuela and other Venezuelan official sources, so they are used interchangeably. When the availability of the Venezuelan sources was not appropriate or satisfactory for some reason, I used the information furnished by the Cepal-Stat or eventually another external official source. When information was collected from ECLAC's annual reports, I used "ECLAC (year)" instead of "Cepal-Stat," the complete reference is mentioned in the list of references at the end of the book. The Cepal-Stat website also has many usable indicators which were elaborated by ECLAC itself. Particularly in Chap. 4, I made use of ECLAC's "National economic and socio-demographic profiles" as an additional tool for elaborating the historical narrative. All websites are mentioned in the references.

The translations from other languages than English were all made by the author. Linear regressions were made using Microsoft Excel, their statistical results being presented in the standard style.

This work benefited from the help and/or commentaries of Alfredo Saad-Filho, Wilson do Nascimento Barbosa, Almudena Cabezas González, and Fabio Luis Barbosa dos Santos. I express my sincere gratitude for their help. I thank particularly Alfredo Saad-Filho for supervising my postdoctoral research at the School of Oriental and African Studies (SOAS) at London, which led to this book, and all the staff at SOAS for their kind support, as well as all the staff at the libraries of the London School of Economics, King's College Archive (Cambridge) and Universidad Complutense de Madrid, where much of the research material was collected. I also thank Steve Ellner for commenting on an earlier version of Chap. 4. The editor Bruno Fiuza and the reviewer at Springer should also be mentioned for all their help and attention with the original manuscript. It should be stressed that all eventual mistakes are entirely the author's responsibility. I also thank all my colleagues at the Federal University of ABC for allowing and supporting my post-doctoral research, particularly Demétrio Gaspari Cirne de Toledo, Muryatan Santana Barbosa, and Paris Yeros, with whom I have discussed some of the ideas presented here. To my partner María Cecilia Ipar and my children Olivia and Valentino, my sincere gratitude for their patience and affection.

Santo André, São Paulo, Brazil Vitor Eduardo Schincariol

Contents

Acronyms and Abbreviations

AD	Acción Democrática
CADIVI	Comissión Nacional de Administración de Divisas (National Comission for Exchange Rate Administration)
CBV	Central Bank of Venezuela
CLAPs	Comités Locales de Abastecimiento y Producción (Local Commitees for Supply and Production)
COPEI	Comité de Organización Política Electoral Independiente
DICOM	Sistema de Divisas de Tipo de Câmbio Complementário Flotante de Mercado (complementary floating exchange rate regime)
DIPRO	Operaciones de Divisas con tipo de câmbio protegido (subsized exchange rate transactions)
ECLAC	Economic Comission for Latin America and the Caribbean
EIA	Energy Information Administration
ERP	Economic Report of the President of the United States
FEDECÁMERAS	Federación de Cámaras y Asociaciones de Comercio y Producción de Venezuela (Venezuelan Federation of Chambers of Commerce)
FONDEN	Fondo para el Desarrollo Nacional (National Fund for Development)
FONDESPA	Fondo para el Desarrollo Económico y Social del País (National Fund for Economic and Social Development)
GDP	Gross Domestic Product
GCF	Gross Capital Formation
IMF	International Monetary Fund
INT	Instituto Nacional de Tierras
LOTTT	Ley Orgánica del Trabajo de los Trabajadores y Trabajadoras (Organic Law of Men and Women Workers)
M1	Monetary aggregate involving cash, checking accounts, traveler's checks, demand deposits, and other checkable deposits

M2	Components of M1 + several less liquid assets as savings deposits, small-denomination time deposits, and balances in retail money of market mutual funds
MUD	Mesa de Unidad Democrática
MVR	Movimiento V República
MBR-200	Movimiento Bolivariano Revolucionário 200
NATO	North Atlantic Treaty Organization
NEP	New Economic Policy
OPEC	Organization of Petroleum Exporting Countries
PDVSA	Petróleos de Venezuela
PDVAL	Productora y Distribuidora Venezolana de Alimentos (Venezuelan Producer and Distributor of Food)
PSUV	Partido Socialista Unificado de Venezuela
RPV	República Bolivariana de Venezuela
SICADI	Sistema Cambiario Alternativo de Divisas (Alternative System of Exchange Rates)
SIMADI	Sistema Marginal de Divisas (Marginal System of Exchange Rates)
TSJ	Tribunal Supremo de Justicia
UN	United Nations
URD	Unión Republicana Democrática
USSR	Union of Soviet Socialist Republics
USA	United States of America

List of Figures

List of Tables

Chapter 1
Venezuela's Historical Background (Twentieth Century)

This chapter will summarize the main aspects of Venezuela's history over the twentieth century, in order to contextualize the historical background that preceded Chávez's ascension over the 1990s. Based on the available literature, it begins with a sketch of the political and social evolution of Venezuela during the last century. The chapter then focuses on some general trends of the economic and social histories of Venezuela since the first oil shock in 1973. A short empirical evaluation of the economic and social data regarding the 1980–1997 interlude is followed, so as to conclude our description of the historical background that preceded and partially explained Hugo Chávez's ascension as a political leader in Venezuela.

1.1 The First Half of the Twentieth Century

The first half of the twentieth century in Venezuela was economically marked by its rise as an oil exporter, by means of a dependent association with international cartels – mainly from the United States – and politically by the dictatorship of General Vicente Gómez, from 1908 to 1935. At this time, Caracas was developing fast, and the state received increasing taxes on oil exports, an increasing level of imports being financed by them. Social institutions were largely maintained with such resources, which were also directed to the army. Enlightened middle classes and urban workers were still marginal to the political game. Power belonged to the state bureaucracy, the army, landowners, and foreign companies.

Juan Vicente Gomez, a typical Latin American *caudillo*, ruled Venezuela under an authoritarian fashion from 1908 until his death in 1935. Gómez's more than 30 years of rule were followed by years of political turmoil, before stabilization from 1958 onward. During his administrations, foreign oil enterprises gained much of their concessions to extract and export Venezuela's crude oil. Gomez had to cope

© The Editor(s) (if applicable) and The Author(s), under exclusive license to Springer Nature Switzerland AG 2020

V. E. Schincariol, *Society and Economy in Venezuela*, SpringerBriefs in Sociology, https://doi.org/10.1007/978-3-030-60083-9_1

with the political opposition arising mainly from the other sectors of the Venezuelan ruling groups.

After his death, the dictator was succeeded by Eleazar López Contreras (1935–1941), former Ministry of War, without free elections. Contreras was another *tachirense*, that is, a fellow supporter of Gomez coming from Táchira (a Venezuelan province). The first period of his administration was on an interim basis (1935–1936). He was elected indirectly in 1936, governing until 1941, under a new constitution (1936). This administration now faced a more heterogeneous opposition, ranging from middle-class liberal groups, students, socialists, and communists. Rómulo Betancourt (1908–1981), who subsequently organized the *Acción Democrática* (AD) party ("Democratic Action"), one of the two most important parties in Venezuela after 1958, became one of the major political figures of the opposition. *Acción Democrática*, which achieved official recognition in 1941, was founded upon a center-left program. Regarding the opposition to Contreras, Ewell observed that:

> The Communist and non-Communist Left continued to collaborate and in October 1936 formed the Partido Democratico Nacional (PDN). Betancourt's allies were suspicious of the Communists but still cooperated with them, openly until Lopez outlawed leftist associations in 1937 and clandestinely for some time thereafter. Foreign affairs also divided the various groups, Betancourt and the Communists supporting the Spanish Republic and Caldera's colleagues endorsing General Francisco Franco. Out of these political associations of the 1930s were to emerge Venezuela's major modern political parties: Betancourt's AD, Gustavo and Eduardo Machado's Partido Comunista de Venezuela (PCV), Caldera's Comite de Organizacion Politica Electoral Independiente (COPEI) and Villaba's Union Republicana Democratica (URD). Active clandestine organization, especially that of Betancourt's AD, enabled the movements to survive and even grow, until Medina lifted the prohibition on political activity. (Ewell 1994, p.418)

Lopez's successor was Isaías Medina Angarita (1897–1953). Angarita, also former Ministry of War, was chosen by the Congress to replace López in 1941, again without free elections. However, he was considered by many as a nationalist and a true democrat. A sympathetic historian observed:

> Although it is true that Medina, a career military man and Minister of War with López Contreras, was an official candidate, elected by indirect vote, it is also true that as soon as his administrative management began, he won the popular will, until he became a symbol of democracy, honesty and ability. Never has a Venezuelan ruler achieved such rapid rise in public opinion and led the State towards prosperity and towards a concept of freedom that the people have always proclaimed. (Morón 2004, 263–264)

Angarita's administration reinforced the existing concessions to foreign oil enterprises operating in Venezuela, particular the American ones, but now under a modernized regulation.[1] Angarita's government continued to face challenges posed

[1] Regarding the state oil policies over this period, Furtado observed: "The new fiscal policy introduced in 1946 […] opened up enormous possibilities for the country. Under the new regulations, oil companies operating in Venezuela paid a royalty per unit of output, a standard income tax and a surtax, the latter having been introduced in 1944. The royalty corresponded to 16 $_{2/3}$ per cent on the value of crude, based on Texan quotations. Taxes could be paid either in money or in petroleum,

by middle-class groups and students, including liberals, communists, and socialists. This broad opposition was centered on a progressive platform, which fought against corruption and demanded free elections, together with the legalization of all political parties. AD's political influence continued to rise among organized labor. Before the Second World War, Angarita oscillated between the Axis powers and the Allies; but in practical terms, Venezuela sided with the Allies, supplying large amounts of oil particularly to the United Kingdom (see Morón 2004, p.264). Venezuela declared war on Germany in February 1945.

As in Brazil during Getúlio Vargas' regime (1930–1945), the new political climate against authoritarianism after the defeat of the Nazi forces contributed to the fall of Angarita, by means of a collaboration particularly between AD and the military. Discontented sectors with what Halperin Donghi called a "complicated system of indirect elections" (Donghi 1975, p.248), led by Rómulo Betancourt, hit the Angarita government in 1945. Rômulo, who had flirted with Marxism, now moderated his aims. A military *junta* took power, Rómulo Betancourt at the head of the new administration. This allowed for the legalization of all political parties, and universal suffrage was created, including women. Rafael Caldera's *Comité de Organización Política Electoral Independiente* (COPEI), the other main political party in Venezuela after 1958, was also recognized and gained influence, acting on a center-right platform. The *junta* ruled until December 1947, when novelist and AD politician Rómulo Gallegos was elected president through free elections.

According to Tarver and Frederick:

> From the onset of the October Revolution -October 18, 1945- until its collapse in November 1948, the country experienced a period of great political change. New parties were formed and democracy was institutionalized by universal, direct, and secret balloting. The previous modernization efforts were revitalized and intensified, thus paving the way for the effective democratization of Venezuelan political life. In economic matters, the *Trienio* (1945–1948), as this time period came to be called, witnessed a process by which capitalism became the only viable road to national development. Additional laws were passed that reinforced the course of modernization at the national level, emphasizing social reform. (Tarver and Frederick 2005, p.99)

However, the higher control by the State of the oil industry after Angarita and a higher degree of democratization and normalization of the Venezuelan political system would not come so soon. Gallegos was deposed on 24 November 1948 by the military, who accused him of not sharing power, particularly with COPEI. The constitution of 1947 was abrogated, and AD and the Communist Party were proscribed. According to the interpretation of Hugo Chávez, Gallegos was in fact overthrown by the *gringos* (i.e., the Americans; see Ramonet 2016, p.115; for a discussion, see also Donghi 1975). But Chávez also claimed that the coup, although supposedly

---

which enabled the State to develop a national oil-refining industry and to participate directly in exports. The Venezuelan government was extremely cautious in its use of this prerogative but fiscal legislation left the possibility open. Income tax was substantially increased in 1946, and in 1948 a further tax was introduced, establishing the principle that profits from the petroleum industry were to be divided on a fifty-fifty basis between the Venezuelan State and the foreign producer companies" (Furtado 1977, p.182.).

maneuvered to favor Washington's interests, had partially failed in its aims, as its leader, Colonel Carlos Delgado Chalbaud, "assumed the Military *Junta* with some progressive tones." Chávez also observed:

> As head of the military Junta, he proceeded to give it a progressive turn, something that was not in Washington's plans. Venezuela was by now an important oil-producing power. And so, Delgado Chalbaud was kidnapped in Caracas in murky circumstances and assassinated on 13 November 1953. A magnicide, in fact. Remember that a few months earlier, in another oil-producing country -Iran- they had ousted Mossadegh" (see Ramonet 2016, p.117)

After Chaubauld's assassination in 1950, Germán Suárez Flemmich assumed as a new interim. Political persecutions were intensified. New elections for a new constituent congress were called for 1952; they occurred, *Unión Republicana Democrática* (UDR) won the elections, but the results were not accepted by the military. UDT's politicians were exiled, and Marcos Pérez Jimenez (affiliated to the *Frente Electoral Independiente* and *Cruzada Cívica Nacionalista* after 1963), a military officer who had participated in the 1945 coup alongside Rómulo Betancourt, assumed the control of the constituent congress, with a new constitution. A new unstable and violent period was initiated, with new disputes among the military and more political proscriptions (particularly for AD and the communists but also for members of COPEI and other groups in the opposition). Marcos Pérez Jiménez was appointed by public opinion as the most beneficiary of Chaubauld's death, according to Ewell (1994, p.748).

During Jiménez's repressive regime, European emigration was increased, and "Americanization" was deepened not only through new agreements and concessions but also through cultural dependence. Caracas expanded, and Venezuela became more urbanized; however, wealth was unequally distributed. Venezuela's economic growth based on oil exports and domestic reinvestment of a share of the oil surplus led the nation to the second rank in terms of GDP growth per capita in Latin America (Argentina being the first; see Bulmer-Thomas 2003, p.300). But agriculture had a poor development as well as other productive sectors (for a discussion, see Bulmer-Thomas 2003, p.300 and Ewell 1994, p.751; for a broad historical account of the period, see Coronil 2002 [1977]).

1.2 From the *Punto Fijo* Pact (1958) to the Neoliberal Crisis

Pérez's oppression, the falling oil prices, and his desire to hold power drove the former antagonistic political groups to the support of one more coup in 1958, once again managed by groups within the army. This time, however, conditions for a longer political stability would be created, under the so-called *Pact of Punto Fijo*, "a pre-electoral agreement by which the leaders of *Unión Republicana Democrática* (URD), Acción Democrática (AD), and the *Comité de Organización Política Electoral Independiente* (COPEI) had pledged to support the winner of the [next] election" (Tarver and Frederick 2005, p.102). A new political period began for

Venezuela. Formal political stability without direct interventions by the military would be achieved for the next decades. Under more or less free elections, political parties would be legalized. AD and COPEI would dominate the political scenario. Rómulo Betancourt, AD's candidate, won the first elections which occurred on 7 November 1958; he governed 5 years long, until new elections in 1963, won by Raúl Leoni, another AD candidate. Betancourt's administration was marked by the creation of the Organization of the Petroleum Exporting Countries (OPEC), which included Venezuela's participation, as well of a new constitution in 1961. Leoni's administration had to cope with guerrilla's activities (such as sabotaging of oil pipelines and bombing of the US embassy in Caracas), as well as an abortive military uprising in October 1966.

Despite the eventual and minor political differences between AD and COPEI and the majority of the other existing political parties, the economy's dependence on oil exports was maintained over the 1970s. This was helped by the boom in oil prices after 1973, which boosted government's receipts. In this context, the government implemented more regulations and taxes, by the introduction of "posted price" system. This sought to stabilize state's receipts in the form of taxes and royalties in the face of the price fluctuations. According to Furtado:

> A law passed in 1970 authorised an increase in taxes and royalties paid by concessionaires. The State's share of the profits of the major operating company (a subsidiary of Standard Oil of New Jersey) increased from 74 per cent in 1969 to 81 per cent in 1971. In addition, the State was empowered to establish posted prices unilaterally and after 1972 the assessment of the operating companies' income was based on posted prices rather than on prices actually *received.* These measures created the conditions for the State to assume complete control over petroleum export prices, a step that was to be taken in 1973 within the framework of the joint action agreed upon with other members of the Organization of Petroleum Exporting Countries (OPEC). (Furtado 1977, p.183)

Relative political stability continued over the period, although communist *guerrillas* maintained their activities in the countryside. Electoral victories were alternated between AD and COPEI under the implicit agreements of the *Punto Fijo* pact. Rafael Caldera Rodriguez, COPEI's candidate, was elected in 1969; he faced strikes in the state sector of the economy and intense political mobilization among the students. He was succeeded by Carlos André Pérez, AD's candidate, in 1973 (both Caldera and Perez would be elected for a second term in 1989 and 1994, respectively). In the context of the first oil shock of 1973, Perez's government created in 1975 a new state oil enterprise, PDVSA (*Petróleos de Venezuela*), so as to absorb the old state firms operating in the sector of extraction and commercialization, as well as the majority of the foreign enterprises over the next years. According to Furtado, who was invited by Venezuela's government to support development and academic projects during this period, the president professed developmental ideas and wanted to take advantage of the higher prices for the oil exports (see Furtado 1997, p.252).

Several factors explained the direction taken toward the progressive nationalization of the whole oil industry. The growing notion of the oil's scarcity as a nonrenewable natural resource has evidently found political echoes in the local leaders, aware of its importance for the country. There were discussions about diminishing returns arising from exhausting of oil fields and on the necessity of diversifying the economic structure, which apparently could be done by the state (for a discussion, see Cano 1999, p.508–511). The perspectives regarding the role that oil should play in Venezuela – that of an "industrializing industry," espoused by Rómulo Betancourt and Juan Pablo Pérez Alfonzo – was added to the conclusions of the Economic Commission for Latin America (ECLAC) regarding the fall in terms of trade and the consequent need for industrialization by means of state policies. The increasing price fluctuations in the international market and its direct repercussions – the same ones that had led to the destabilization of Pérez Jimenez – also pointed toward a progressive control by the state.

However, after the new difficult conditions regarding oil exports from 1980 onward, PDVSA began to operate under conditions of increasing autonomy in the face of the domestic crisis. The path of nationalization clashed with falling external demand in the United States. After 1980, PDVSA subsequently reduced production, also because of the supply limitation agreements within the OPEC. As a means to offset the declining demand and the investments by foreign companies in the face of the nationalization, PDVSA increased its investments abroad through acquisitions in the United States, Germany, and many other nations. The delinking of its activities regarding the Venezuelan economy would be severely criticized, being a partial failure of the developmental goals that existed around its foundation by the mid-1970s. Chávez, particularly after the coup attempt in 2002, would frequently repeat that PDVSA had become a "state within the state," its investments and profits abroad creating jobs outside Venezuela and its associations with the international cartels maintaining Venezuela's dependence under new conditions. This was a common critique of PDVSA's operations by the left economists in Venezuela (see Martins 2007 and Mommer 2001 for critical discussions).

At the beginning of the 1980s, the economic and social situation was deteriorating. The public sector saw a drop in net revenues. Venezuela's population grew by 1.44 times between 1970 and 1983.[2] Accordingly, the rate of unemployment, which reached only 6% in 1980, more than doubled in 5 years, reaching 13% by 1985. Minimum wages dropped by an average of 25% over the same period and at the end of the decade reached only 60% of its original values in 1980.[3] President Herrera Campins, COPEI's leader, elected in 1978, had to cope with falling prices of oil after 1980 and social unrest, *guerrilla* activities still existing. He declared: "I have found an unbalanced economy, a great structural disequilibrium, speculative inflationary pressures, [which] harmed the middle classes and marginal groups in the nation. I have found a mortgaged nation" (quoted by Chávez Frías 2013, vol. 1, p.400). On 4 October 1983, the army killed 23 members of the "Américo Silva" guerrilla movement in the province of Anzoátegui (the "Cantaura massacre").

[2] See Cepal-Stat, Venezuela, "Total population by sex."

[3] See Cepal-Stat, Venezuela, "Real minimum wages, 2000 = 100" and "Unemployment rates by sex."

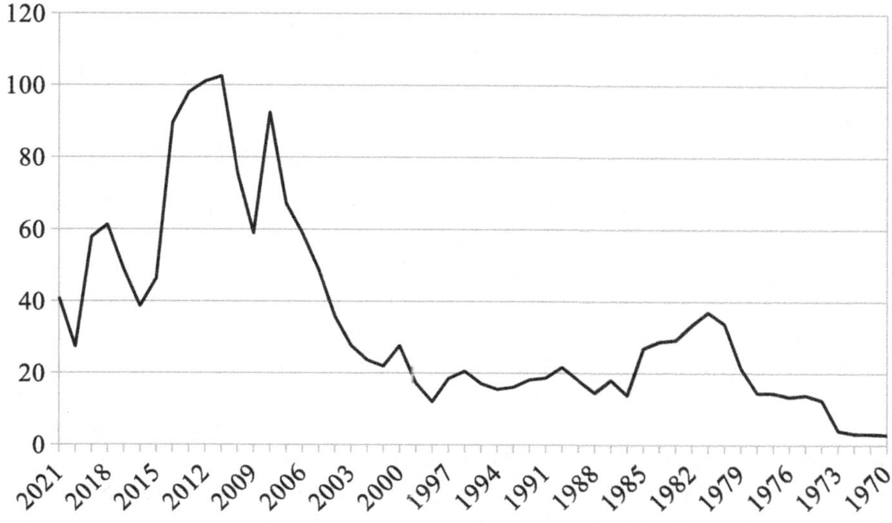

Fig. 1.1 The United States imported crude oil prices per barrel since 1968, including previsions for 2020–2021. US$ dollars. (Source: US Energy Information Administration)

During the presidency of Jaime Lusinchi (AD, elected in December 1983), some important works of infrastructure were finished, as the hydroelectric power plants of Guri and San Agatón, but as the current account of the balance of payments faced decreasing surpluses from 1980 to 1985 (reaching deficits from 1986 until 1989), there was a permanent pressure on the fixed exchange rate regime.[4] On 18 February 1983, the Bolívar was devaluated from 4.30 to 7.50/1US$ (the so-called Black Friday). Facing the domestic downturn, PDVSA invested outside the nation. Venezuela's total direct investments abroad reached US$ 460 million in 1986, 20% of the total exports over the same year.[5] After two decades of a fixed exchange rate regime, the Central Bank introduced controls and two different rates for the dollar. According to the Energy Information Administration (EIA), the physical sales of oil to the United States stagnated until 1990, under a fall in prices which were not interrupted until 1990–1991, during the Gulf War (see Fig. 1.1). In this context, another political massacre occurred on 8 May 1986, when members of the "Bandera Roja" [Red Flag] political organization were murdered by state agents.

In this context, Former President Carlos André Pérez (AD) was reelected on 4 December 1988 with 52% of the votes; the COPEI candidate received 40%. Pérez, whose first administration had implemented the nationalization of the oil industry and behaved in a nationalist and "developmentalist" fashion, now sided with those who argued for reforms. The worsening of the social and economic conditions led to riots and a brutal repression by the state forces during the so-called Caracazo in February 1989. State repression led to hundreds of deaths, including children. This

[4] See Cepal-Stat, Venezuela, "External sector." Deficits reached US$ 5.8 billion in 1988.

[5] See Cepal-Stat, Venezuela, "External sector."

created a tremendous psychological impact and Pérez was destabilized. The president reacted with the suspension of constitutional rights, including a curfew. In December, there was a high abstention and gains for the left parties in the elections for province governments.

On 20 March 1990, Venezuela reached an agreement with the International Monetary Fund, which involved privatizations, trade liberalization, lower state subsidies, and the end of the exchange rate controls. The estimated initial amounts involved US$ 1.899 million.[6] Gasoline prices were raised as well as tariffs for the public transports; the *Bolívar* suffered a maxi-devaluation. By September 1991, 45% of stocks of the state airline *Viasa* were sold to the Spanish enterprise *Iberia* and 15% to the *Provincial* bank. The government started to talk more openly about a so-called *apertura petrolera*, that is, the "opening" of the oil production to foreign investments. Agreements and partnerships with foreign groups would be started so as to explore new oil fields and to create mixed enterprises. These agreements would begin by 1995. Oil royalties would be reduced from 16% to 1%, as tax evasion was intensified (see Martins 2007). The nationalist tide was fading away, PDVSA gained more autonomy, and the economy was being more internationalized again. Social tensions continued, reflected in then Colonel Hugo Chávez and MBR-200's [*Revolutionary Bolivarian Movement* – 200][7] further attempt of a military coup on 4 February 1992. Pérez suspended some measures, reintroducing price controls for food and medicine. By November 1992, another attempt to overthrow Pérez was made by other rebels within the army; Constitution was suspended.

Even with a better performance of the GDP and unemployment rates between 1990 and 1992, Pérez was weakened by this succession of crises; he was then brought on trial by the Senate, being accused of corruption. Pérez was suspended from office and Senator Ramón José Velasquez (independent) assumed power as an interim president until the elections on 5 December 1993, won by Former President Rafael Caldera and his new party, *Convergencia*, created by dissidents of the COPEI and supported by a share of the left forces. This was the first time since 1958 that nor AD nor COPEI won a presidential election. However, despite the initial hopes that Caldera could have implemented an alternative policy, the new president began to endorse the alleged necessity for more neoliberal reforms.

Excluding the brief recovery of the social and economic conditions between 1989 and 1991, the situation was deteriorating again, which included a serious crisis in the *Latino* bank by January 1992; the Central Bank intervened. According to the ECLA, unemployment rates, which reached 6% in 1993, would hit 8% in 1994 and 10% in 1995; real minimum wages dropped again. Gross capital formation, private consumption, and imports were all falling or stagnated since 1992; oil prices declined again in foreign markets, the oil barrel being sold for less than 20 dollars (see next section).

---

[6] See Cepal-Stat, Venezuela, "Use of IMF credit and loans and exceptional financing." The last installments involving the IMF resources to Venezuela over the period would be paid during Chávez's first administration.

[7] Simón Bolívar was born in Caracas on 24 July 1783.

Caldera's administration sought more credits from the International Monetary Fund, these policies being coordinated by former *guerrillero* and now Minister of Planning Teodoro Petkoff. *The New York Times* announced on 13 July 1996:

> Announcing the loan, the I.M.F. spoke approvingly of Venezuela's 'ambitious and front-loaded economic program.' It said the program was designed to redress a dismal economic situation in this potentially rich oil-producing country, which has suffered slow growth, 57 percent inflation, a big budget deficit and difficulties in the banking sector. Under the new program, Venezuela has already lifted price controls on all goods except medicine as well as controls on currency flows in and out of the country and on interest rates. It is now committed to cutting public spending steeply, strengthening its banks and selling off state-owned telecommunications, aluminum, steel, electrical and petrochemical plants. (*The New York Times*, Section 1, July 1996, p.13)

Caldera then implemented as he could the IMF's agenda. The Bank of Venezuela and Bank *Consolidado* were sold to Spain's *Santander* and Chile's *Corp Group*. Mobil, Veba Öl, and Nippon Oil gained authorization to extract oil from the Venezuelan soil by January 1995. But the social conditions were not sufficiently ameliorated. The ongoing economic and social difficulties under the last 2 years of Caldera's administration would benefit the emergence of new left-wing political groups, now guided by Chávez, who had been liberated from jail by March 1994 amidst great popular manifestations. He started to organize the so-called *Comités Bolivarianos* ["Bolivarian Committees"] on a national basis; after discussions with the other members of the MBR-200, it was decided that Chávez would be running for the next presidential elections.

1.3 A Short Empirical Overview (1980–1998)

This section gives a short summary of the evolution of the economic and social conditions over the 1980–1998 period, which preceded Chávez's election in 1998, relying on the available data released by the ECLA, which, in some cases, cover the period 1980–1997.[8]

We shall begin with some theoretical remarks. Regarding the above mentioned process of external indebtedness in Venezuela and other peripheral nations after 1973, Joan Robinson observed: "There is no magic in 'importing capital' that can be relied upon to generate development unless the digestive mechanism of the recipient is able to make use of it" (Robinson 1979, p.86). Unfortunately, Venezuela's institutional framework at that moment did not show proper conditions for this "digestive mechanism." Celso Furtado's pioneer approach of Venezuela's condi-

[8]The majority of the available statistics and indicators on ECLA's website cover the 1990–2015 period for the whole of Latin America, Venezuela included. The same cannot be said about Venezuela's official websites, which lack organization or more specific data on the 1980–1990 period. ECLAC's website has also the advantage of displaying all the available data on the same link. See https://cepalstat-prod.cepal.org/.

tions helps to understand why. His work on the Venezuelan economy and particularly on its limits to development on the basis of oil exports is still one of the most advanced in the field of economic development and deserves to be revisited.

Furtado visited Venezuela during and after his work at the ECLA. Working with a team of local researchers, he made an independent estimation of the main economic aggregates of Venezuela for 1945–1956 (see Furtado 2008, p.83–118). Beyond his many works on the Latin American economic development at that time, he tackled the "structural" features of the Venezuelan economy in two specific articles: *Estudio de la economía venezuelana, 1957* (Economic study of Venezuela, 1957), an extremely sophisticated and realist approach which he has never published in life, and *Notas sobre a economia venezuelana e suas perspectivas atuais* (Some notes on the Venezuelan economy and its present perspectives), which Furtado firstly published as a chapter of his autobiography (Furtado 1997) and which contains his estimation of the Venezuelan main macroeconomic aggregates. Both works are now published in a collection of his studies on Venezuela (Furtado 2008).

Furtado saw Venezuela as a very atypical case of an underdeveloped nation, which enjoyed (at that time) a high domestic supply of foreign reserves. Extraction and export of crude oil were responsible for 25% of the GDP, but only 3% of the total employment. The Central Bank bought dollars coming from the oil exports made by the foreign enterprises and sold them for profit remittances. Up to that moment, this mechanism fostered overvalued rates of exchange and a high propensity to import, ranging from food to modern equipment. This process led to unemployment by means of a high capital product rate in the overall economy, helped also by a high population growth. However, as the inflow of external resources increased, the freedom to implement political policies also did, in theoretical terms; the state tended to invest in infrastructure works, which boosted temporarily employment rates but which did not create a permanent flow of wealth when finished, nor exports.

However, in practical terms, Furtado argues that there was a great *inertial* mechanism in Venezuela and practical limits to the state actions, oil extraction sectors having "its own dynamics" and state policies being also influenced by those who benefited from that type of institutional arrangement which did not led automatically to economic development (Furtado 2008, p.120). Domestic aggregate savings were extremely low, as well as taxes as a share of the GDP (one of the lowest in Latin America). The high level of reserves stimulated the imports of modern machines and so a low domestic manufacturing production outside oil extraction, which reinforced the structural unemployment of the economy. The nation had a high rate of inequality, but as subsidies to consumption were made mainly through imports, domestic agriculture was weak. This feature was intensified by the specific conditions of the majority of the Venezuelan tropical soil, cultivated through the techniques of shifting cultivation, marked by periodical interruptions and the relatively poor quality of land in many areas. Even with some land reforms being introduced, these faced the inability of peasants and the difficulties related to the cultivation of small and medium plots of land.

The point is that oil abundance and higher prices for oil were not an easy solution. They stimulated a high coefficient of imports, reducing the domestic multiplier effects for the economy as a whole coming from domestic investments. In light of that, higher prices and an abundance of foreign reserves demanded a resolute action by the state in order to avoid the accumulation of structural heterogeneities, as well as aggregate imbalances and the dependent internationalization of the economy. The patterns of demand should be altered, attacking the consumption of luxury goods and the mere imitation of foreign patterns of consumption which required economic inequality. Taxes should encourage labor-using techniques in order to counterbalance the tendency of importing modern capital. Public works should also be encouraged to absorb the surplus population which was growing also due to the high rates of fertility. There had been some additional industrialization outside oil extraction, but this was a "complementary one," which did not reduce the dependence of imports as a whole. This industrialization should be deepened, toward a higher level of autonomy, which was theoretically possible given the abundance of natural resources, finance, and capacity to import.

This is a sketch of Furtado's groundbreaking analysis for the 1957–1970 interlude. Looking retrospectively in 1974, he already believed that "the opportunity to jump over underdevelopment was lost" (Furtado 2008, p.265). He observed that the tax rate system had not been reformed and subsidies were still maintained through food imports and free gasoline. Autonomous and diversified industrialization had not been achieved; there was a high waste of reserves in the form of luxury goods and exports of the domestic savings. This condition of underdevelopment where state resources depended mainly on oil exports still acted as an inertial mechanism that prevented, by means of an accommodation process, a higher diversification of the economy (the so-called *rentismo*). Given that, most of the trade surpluses in oil exports were being wasted in unproductive imports of consumption goods; despite the creation of PDVSA, the unproductive character of the economy had not been altered. The government, traders, and domestic private enterprises all got loans from abroad. Given the developmentalism mood of the middle 1970s, the government nationalized the oil production and other industries such as mining, but imports increased, and domestic production in the overall economy outside oil extraction, services, and infrastructure was curtailed or postponed.

This would not be the end of the history for Venezuela, but according to Furtado – and he seemed to be right – the authorities did not take a proper advantage of the enormous inflow of resources that came from the oil shock of 1973, which reinstated the abovementioned condition of a high supply of foreign reserves. This condition would disappear with the crisis of the external debt over the 1980s. Having this characterization in mind, we shall now turn to some of the empirical aspects of the economy after 1980. One main historical change after Furtado's analysis was related to the crisis in the balance of payments, which eliminated the abundance of foreign reserves. Figure 1.1 shows prices for the imported oil in the United States, which reflected the general conditions for oil exports in Venezuela. The oil market saw better prices between 1973 and 1979, which led to a fivefold increase in total export gains. These gains were almost matched by a similar increase in imports.

State's resources were improved, and the economy grew under those "dependent" conditions also formulated in the classic work of Cardoso and Faletto, who argued that even though external dependence on foreign markets provided for some "modernization" and domestic economic growth, structural imbalances and particularly the unequal distribution of wealth were maintained (see Cardoso and Faletto 1979).[9]

The performance in oil exports over the 1970s, which led to an easier condition regarding foreign reserves, induced a new process of foreign indebtedness. Given rising foreign reserves, external indebtedness did not seem a problem. On the side of the supply of capital, the higher oil prices after 1973 created a huge amount of resources in the international finance system, now available to underdeveloped nations under low rates of interest until 1979. Venezuela, and other oil exporters as Mexico, would apparently benefit from higher oil prices through new foreign loans.[10] Domestic traders, banks, and the Venezuelan government all took advantage of the apparently favorable conditions in external money markets. But after the monetary shock in interest rates by the Federal Reserve in 1979 (which intended to stop the American inflation rates as well as the devaluation of the dollar), the borrowers, including the oil exporters, ended up with huge amounts of foreign debts, despite a new rise in oil prices in the same year (for an overall account of the Latin American economic performance over the 1980s, see Ffrench-Davis 1994).

Table 1.1 shows data for the Venezuelan balance of payments between 1990 and 1998. After the rise in interest rates and the fall in oil prices after 1980, Venezuela, together with the majority of its Latin American counterparts, faced a new economic crisis. The crisis arose from the fact that oil prices dropped and international interest rates were higher after 1979; this led to fiscal crisis and the exportation of a higher share of the domestic surplus, preventing new investments and the expansion of the domestic economy, even under "dependent" features (i.e., exports leading to a moderate domestic growth without structural changes in the socioeconomic conditions). As Table 1.1 shows, between 1980 and 1983, exports dropped from 19 to US$ 14 billion, but imports were still on the rise. Physical extraction of oil declined until 1985, recovering in partial terms between 1985 and 1990. Exports and imports then dropped together until 1989, but imports continued to be a large share of exports (90% in 1986, 83% in 1987, and in fact exceeding exports in 1988).

Balance on income (net results on employment compensations and investment incomes [direct investments, portfolio, and other investments]) reached dramatic negative levels between 1983 and 1985, expressing high interest payments. Net autonomous capital inflows were negative until 1987, denoting a low domestic

[9]While modernization and dependent industrialization, here in the form of oil extraction and its indirect impacts on the domestic economy, "intensified the exclusive social system characteristic of capitalism in peripheral communities, it nonetheless promoted capital accumulation and increasing complexity in the production structure" (Cardoso and Faletto 1979, p.159).

[10]Coronil observed: "It is ironic that a state that constitutes itself as a national state through the control over its petroleum has been broken [*deshecho*] when using the nations's subsoil [*subsuelo*] as a guarantee of contracted loans to finance an industrial development project designed to put an end to oil dependence" (Coronil 2002 [1977], p.435).

Table 1.1 Venezuela. Balance of payments, 1980–1998

Years	Exports	Imports	Balance on current account	Balance on income	Income (debts)	Net autonomous capital inflows	Direct investment in Venezuela	Global balance	Net resource transfers to the world
1980	19,275	10,877	4728	329	-1935.0	−965.1	55.0	3762	−636.1
1981	20,181	12,123	4000	574	−3007.0	−4021.5	184.0	−21	−3447.5
1982	16,516	13,584	−4246	530	−4095.0	−3914.0	257.0	−8160	−5444.0
1983	14,759	6409	4427	−2113	−3613.0	−3981.0	86.0	446	−6094.0
1984	16,075	7246	4651	−2062	−4155.0	−3014.7	18.0	1636	−5076.7
1985	14,478	7501	3327	−2233	−4143.0	−1627.5	68.0	1699	−3860.5
1986	8664	7866	−2245	602	−3358.0	−1636.5	16.0	- 3881	−3238.5
1987	10,564	8870	−1390	619	−3067.0	455.0	21.0	−935	−1164.0
1988	10,217	12,080	−5809	771	−3416.0	1937.0	89.0	−3872	166.0
1989	13,059	7365	2161	−2368	−3950.0	−2047.4	213.0	113	−3451.8
1990	17,623	6917	8279	−774	−3422.0	−5803.1	451.0	2475	−4677.3
1991	15,159	10,259	1736	−598	−2758.0	688.4	1916.0	2424	311.3
1992	14,202	12,880	−3749	746	−3350.0	3087.3	629.0	−661	1158.4
1993	14,779	11,504	−1993	715	−3311.0	2117.2	372.0	124	134.0
1994	16,092	8424	2541	904	−3530.0	−3485.1	801.0	−944	−5590.4
1995	19,068	12,007	2014	943	−3810.0	−3458.2	996.0	−1444	−5864.2
1996	23,692	9881	8914	725	−3304.0	−2675.8	2183.0	6238	−4367.7
1997	23,871	14,917	3732	−2517	NA	−141.0	6202.0	3591	−2658.0
1998	17,707	16,755	−4432	−2534	NA	1543.0	4985.0	−2889	−991.0

Selected indicators. US millions
Source: Cepal-Stat

growth and the dangers of investing in a nation which faced shortage of foreign reserves. The current account of the balance of payments suffered a decline between 1985 and 1989, deficits between 1986 and 1989, and new deficits between 1991 and 1993. The global results of the balance of payments were negative or stagnated, amidst negative net transfers of resources to the world reaching an average of US$ 3/5 billion per year. It should be also mentioned that the available statistics do not mention any positive values for the inflow of income on direct investments of Venezuela abroad (mainly from PDVSA) until 1986 (when they reached only US$ 5 million). These values reached US$ 68 million by 1988, US$ 231 million in 1990, and US$ 347 million in 1990 but disappeared from the official data for the balance of payments since 1994. There were net resources transfers to the world over the whole period (with the exception of 1988 and between 1991 and 1993), a path which explains the difficulties involving the public finance and the domestic rate of investment.

The available official statistics for the domestic economy show other aspects of the worsening economy over the 1980–1997 period. High imports led to a relative drop of the manufacturing sectors regarding the GDP, from 21% in 1984 to 19% in

Table 1.2 Venezuela. System of national accounts

Years	Manufacturing	Agriculture	Mining, including oil	Finance and real estate	Trade, repairing, restaurants, hotels	Public administration
1984	0.21	0.05	0.16	0.14	0.15	0.14
1985	0.22	0.06	0.14	0.13	0.15	0.14
1986	0.23	0.07	0.09	0.15	0.17	0.15
1987	0.21	0.06	0.12	0.13	0.17	0.14
1988	0.21	0.07	0.11	0.14	0.19	0.14
1989	0.21	0.06	0.18	0.12	0.18	0.12
1990	0.21	0.05	0.23	0.11	0.17	0.11
1991	0.20	0.05	0.18	0.12	0.18	0.13
1992	0.19	0.05	0.16	0.12	0.19	0.13
1993	0.18	0.05	0.15	0.13	0.19	0.13
1994	0.17	0.05	0.17	0.16	0.18	0.13
1995	0.17	0.05	0.15	0.15	0.18	0.13
1996	0.18	0.04	0.22	0.12	0.15	0.11
1997	0.16	0.04	0.17	0.13	0.15	0.14
1998	0.14	0.05	0.10	0.15	0.16	0.18

Selected indicators (GDP = 1.00). 1984–1998. Current *Bolívares* of 1984
Source: Cepal-Stat

1992; manufacturing showed further losses in terms of the GDP until 1997. Agriculture stagnated in relative terms, as well as public administration. The agriculture production indices per head grew by approximately 10% between 1970 and 1980 but dropped between 1980 and 1984 and again between 1987 and 1994.[11] Food production per head, which also grew by approximately 10% over the 1970s, dropped all over the 1980s, excluding 1986 and 1988. Its performance during the 1990s is erratic, showing a clear drop between 1992–1996[12] (Table 1.2).

Financial intermediation and real estate also dropped in relative terms over the 1980s, which showed falling foreign investments in finance sectors and their corresponding impacts on real estate financial conditions, together with the drop in foreign reserves. Unproductive sectors, which were not affected by imports but which could not *export*, operated as substitutes for manufacturing investments (such as trade, repairing, restaurants, hotels), being all increased in terms of the GDP. Mining, which here means mainly oil extraction, came down in the first half of the 1980s, under the falling prices for oil between 1980 and 1985, recovering at the end of the decade as prices were partially improved (such as shown by Fig. 1.1). The relative share of oil extraction in the economy in fact oscillated under the fluctuations of the oil prices and international demand over the following years, show-

[11] See Cepal-Stat, Venezuela, "Agricultural production indices per capita."

[12] See Cepal-Stat, Venezuela, "Food production indices per capita."

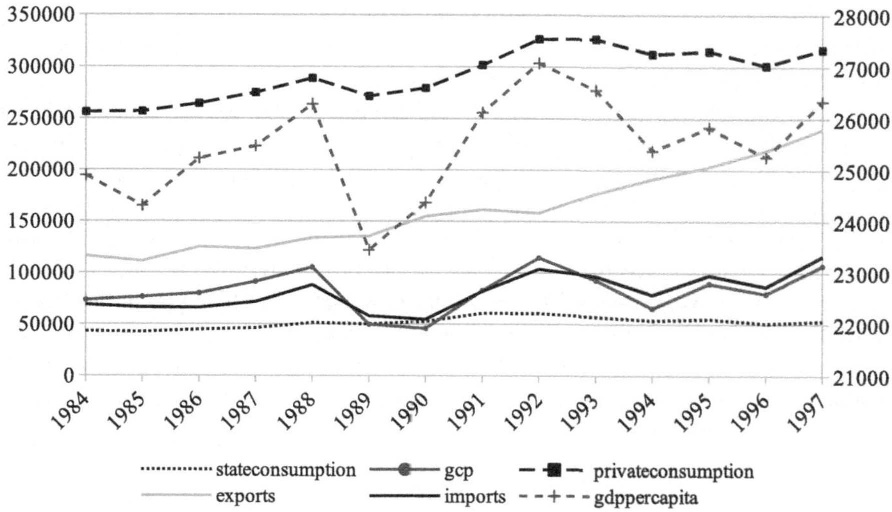

Fig. 1.2 Venezuela. GDP by sectors. Selected indicators. 1984–1997. Constant *Bolívares* (millions) of 1984. (Source: Cepal-Stat. GDP per capita estimated by the annual GDP divided by total population as informed by Cepal-Stat. Observation: GDP per capita on the right axis)

ing a downward trend which is related to stagnated prices until the beginning of the 2000s.

Figure 1.2 shows the macroeconomic patterns of the economy over the 1984–1997 period.

The data shows the great stability of state expenditures over time, even when exports started to recover more strongly since 1990. This is because a relevant share of the state's resources was expended in subsidies to consumption and because the tax system remained poor. Investments (gross capital formation) showed two drops, linked to the adjustment policies of "reform" adopted by the second administrations of Pérez and then Caldera. Subsidies were made partially through imports, its share in the GDP being raised from 16% to 19% between 1984 and 1997. This rise in imports was also explained by the loss of the domestic manufacturing production and the incapacity to prevent the inflow of imports at a given state of demand, related not only to subsidies but also to luxury consumption and intermediate goods. It is an underdeveloped feature of the economy the fact that the share of exports was raised from 27% to 39% of the GDP, while the GDP per capita was showing two sharp declines and social conditions were worsening. The large rise in imports over time evidently caused a significant damage to the local production of tangible goods and, apart from helping to lower inflation rates, had no economic rationale for a nation whose external debt reached 75% of the GDP in 1990.

Venezuela's erratic trajectory during the 1980–1997 interlude was reflected in its social conditions. It is in general accepted that violence spread rapidly in the urban areas and that poverty aggravated. The Gini coefficient for wealth distribution shows this deterioration, reaching 0.471 by 1990, 0.486 in 1994, and 0.507 in 1989,[13] a clear sign that 15 years of decreasing economic growth coupled with rising unemployment worsened the social conditions in the nation. This scenario created the conditions for the political changes represented by Chávez and his political movement, which would rehabilitate the developmental approach for Venezuela now under a socialist-oriented basis. Chávez's victory in 1998 represented the end of the political conditions established by the *Punto Fijo* pact. After being paid, IMF loans would not be renewed during his presidency, as Venezuela's total extern debt was lowered from 75% of the GDP in 1989 to 43% in 1998 and only 21% in 2008[14] under a new boom in commodities and specially in oil markets.[15] A new historical period would begin in Venezuela.

References

Agénor PR, Montiel PJ (2018) Development macroeconomics, 4th edn. Princeton University Pres, Princeton

Bulmer-Thomas V (2003) The economic history of Latin America since Independence. Cambridge University Press, Cambridge, UK

Cano W (1999) Soberania e política econômica na América Latina. Edunesp, São Paulo

Cardoso FH, Faletto E (1979) Dependency and development in Latin America. University of California Press, Berkeley

Chávez Frías H (2013) Discursos del Presidente ante la Asamblea Nacional (1999–2012), vol I–IV. Feditorial de la Assemblea Nacional William Lara, Caracas

Coronil F (2002 [1977]) El Estado mágico. Naturaleza, dinero y modernidad en Venezuela. Nueva Sociedad, Caracas

Donghi TH (1975) História da América Latina. Paz e Terra, Rio de Janeiro

Ewell J (1994) Venezuela since 1930. In: Bethell L (ed) The Cambridge history of Latin America, vol VIII. Cambridge University Press, Cambridge, UK

Ffrench-Davis R (1994) The Latin American economies, 1950-1990. In: Bethell L (ed) The Cambridge history of Latin America, vol VI. Cambridge University Press, Cambridge, UK

Furtado C (1977) Economic development of Latin America. Cambridge Economic Press, Cambridge, UK

Furtado C (1997) Obra autobiográfica Tomo III. Paz e Terra, Rio de Janeiro

[13] See Cepal-Stat, Venezuela, "Gini Coefficient."

[14] See Cepal-Stat, Venezuela, "Total external debt as a percentage of the GDP."

[15] "For most developing countries the decade of the 2000s had been a prosperous one up to that point, with many countries experiencing rapid growth, low inflation, and favorable performance in their external accounts. Those positive outcomes were the results of the structural and macroeconomic reforms implemented during the 1990s as well as a very favorable external environment. Macroeconomic stabilization issues therefore tended to move to the background of policy concerns, giving way to concerns with structural issues such as poverty and income distribution, unemployment, reform of the legal system and the civil service, and improvements in accountability and transparency of government operations" (Agénor and Montiel 2018, p. xix).

Furtado C (2008) Ensaios sobre a Venezuela: subdesenvolvimento com abundância de di- visas. Contraponto, Rio de Janeiro
Martins CE (2007) Venezuela. In: Sader E, Jinkings I (eds) Enciclopédia Contemporânea da América Latina e do Caribe. Boitempo, São Paulo
Mommer B (2001) Venezuela, política y petróleos. In: Valecillos H, Bello O (eds) La economía contemporánea de Venezuela. Central Bank of Venezuela, Caracas
Morón G (2004) Historia contemporánea de Venezuela. Ciudad de México, Fondo de Cultura Económica
Ramonet I Hugo Chávez (2016) My first life, conversations with Hugo Chávez. Verso, London
Robinson J (1979) Aspects of development and underdevelopment. Cambridge University Press, Cambridge
Tarver HM, Frederick JC (2005) The history of Venezuela. Greenwood Press, London

Chapter 2
Socialism: The Legacies of History and Chávez's Perspectives

Since 2003, the government policies in Venezuela officially declared to pursue socialist goals. According to Hugo Chávez, the struggle for socialism should be maintained over this new century. But he argued that there should be a new type of a socialism which should take into account the Venezuelan historical and intellectual traditions, as well as the limits and dangers of adopting foreign models, particularly the Soviet style of economic policies. This chapter tackles the question of the legacies of socialism at the end of the twentieth century and how Chávez interpreted them. The chapter firstly shows some of the modern theoretical perspectives on socialist planning and its reform attempts and in light of that approaches Hugo Chávez's ideas on socialism. The chapter then tackles Chávez's Bolivarian Doctrine and his thoughts on socialism; this is followed by an appreciation in light of the history of socialism. This historical reflection will be important in order to understand the economic policies adopted in Venezuela after 1998, including some of their shortcomings.

2.1 Reforming Socialism

The first experience of a socialist economy without a full socialization of the means of production and control of the workforce allocation occurred by reasons of radical historical circumstances during the New Economic Policy (NEP) in the USSR (1921–1928). As we know, in face of the destruction caused by the civil war, the Bolsheviks saw the introduction of a complete socialist planning as unfeasible, private markets being allowed to work until the introduction of the first 5-year plan (1928–1932). The experience and the literature on socialist planning had further developments with G. Feldman, A. Preobrazhensky, and other Soviet economists. Outside the USSR, the literature on socialist planning was also developed in the works of M. Kalecki, M. Ellman, M. Dobb, and Y. Tinbergen (for a summing up of

© The Editor(s) (if applicable) and The Author(s), under exclusive license to Springer Nature Switzerland AG 2020

V. E. Schincariol, *Society and Economy in Venezuela*, SpringerBriefs in Sociology, https://doi.org/10.1007/978-3-030-60083-9_2

the literature, see Nove and Nuti 1972). Following 1945, the capitalist world also implemented nationalizations, as well as partial and/or indicative state planning (see Furtado 1977, Hobsbawm 1994, and Pons and Service 2010).

The idea of *reforming* a centrally planned economy through the introduction or permission of private enterprises and mobility of the labor force dates back to the 1960s, in the Eastern Europe as well as the USSR (see Nove 1992; Kornai 2008). There were already some theoretical arguments for that. For example, Oskar Lange had developed over the 1930s a theoretical model of a dual economic system, where consumption goods would be sold at market prices, while capital goods would still be controlled by the planning commission (Lange 1936). Despite being a controversial theme in the USSR, some attempts were made to introduce market mechanisms particularly in Hungary and in Yugoslavia, where collectively managed enterprises were allowed to take their own decisions regarding prices, investment decisions, and even the selection of clients (for a contemporary appreciation, see Fürst et al. 2017; see also Eatwell et al. 1990). These discussions were also made in China and Cuba, leading to different achievements (China distancing itself over time, Cuba remaining loyal to the Soviet model). Linear algebra and other mathematical methods were then developed by L. Kantorovich so as to improve state planning (see Kantorovich 1965; Wilczynski 1972), even though conclusions pointed to an increasing difficulty of planning as the modern socialist economy became more complex over time (see Robinson and Eatwell 1973; Nove 1992). In light of that, the general conclusion was that a socialist economy should in fact implement some kind of decentralized decisions and allow for some private market incentives in order to achieve more "intensive" and not only "extensive" growth (see Brus 1973; Wilczynski 1972; Laski and Brus 1991, and Ellman 2014). In other words, the stage of a so-called primitive socialist accumulation, when forced industrialization should took place to build the material preconditions for socialism,[1] should give place to a second stage, by means of a "major institutional change that replaced the traditional model of a socialist economy by an alternative model of a socialist economy that combined centralised state decision making with a market mechanism" (Ellman 2014, p.52). However, these discussions focused mainly on the already existing socialist economies of that time and less on agrarian or "developing" nations trying to implement socialism by "democratic" means. In the Venezuelan recent case, this difference included (1) the absence of an international socialist camp, (2) the absence of the political monopoly of the socialist party in power,[2] and (3) the absence of the public ownership of the majority of the means of production.

The discussions on a market socialism had an impact on the course of the Soviet and Chinese histories during the 1980s, particularly with Gorbachev's search for

[1] That is, "[a] high level of forced savings extracted from the population, especially the peasants, in a backward country in transition from capitalism to socialism, designed to finance rapid industrialization. The idea and the term were introduced by E. Preobrazhensky in the USSR in the early 1920s" (Wilczynski 1981, p.456).

[2] As Yaffe observed, "the Venezuelan electoral system has brought forward a radically new government, but not an entirely new state or social relations" (Yaffe 2015, p.24).

"glasnost" and "perestroika" and the Chinese adoption of private markets in agriculture, as well as the acceptance of foreign capitalist investments in specific sectors of the economy (see Ellman and Kontorovich 1992 and Brown 2009). The loss of control of the events in the Soviet Union at the beginning of the 1990s and the subsequent reintroduction of capitalism in all the former socialist camp, including African nations where socialist liberation forces had won the war over the European colonialism, led to an abandonment of almost all discussions concerning a socialist economy and socialist planning, North Korea and Cuba being the last remnants of the old model of full state planning.

At the same time, the long-run effects of the international crisis of 1971–1973 on the so-called socialist camp, particularly on their balance of payments, prevented eventual positive results arising from those reforms. In fact it is impossible to detach completely the failures of the socialist economies from their domestic political scenarios and also the broader international conditions of the 1970s and 1980s, particularly in Eastern Europe. The majority of the former socialist nations – particularly Yugoslavia, Poland, and the Socialist Germany – had significant economic ties with the West. The drop in the economic growth of the main capitalist economies over 1973–1982 led to falling exports and external indebtedness in the socialist side. At the same time, socialism had been imposed by the Soviet Union on the majority of the Eastern Europe after 1945, having been never fully accepted by the (conservative) majority of the populations in the region, despite the progressive achievements of the socialist model (for a discussion, see Mazower 1999 and Barbosa 2017). In light of that, it could be argued that those theoretical formulations toward a "reformed" socialist economy without a full state planning did not have economic or even social conditions to be implemented, particularly following the rise of the aggressive Western policies toward the USSR after Ronald Reagan and Margaret Thatcher.

Thus, after 1991, socialism apparently became an issue for historians, being treated with growing contempt and cynicism. Former communist and socialist parties adhered to social democracy or even neoliberalism (one of the extreme cases was given by some Italian ex-communists which once in power supported NATO's bombing of Yugoslavia). Some important features of socialist planning were still retained in China (strong presence of state planning and the political monopoly of the Communist Party), but the rapid growth of capitalist property and inequality in this nation did not contribute to ameliorate the socialist demoralization after 1991, China being frequently defined as more capitalist than socialist (for a discussion, see Tomba 2010 and Piketty 2019). By its turn, Cuba, North Korea, and the remaining African socialist nations did not have the geopolitical or economic power to influence the events on a world scale; their economic difficulties as isolated nations helped to disseminate the capitalist propaganda.

Thus, after the end of the USSR and the practical conversion of China into a predominantly mixed economy (if so), even the quest for a market socialism was questioned, such as in the neo-Hayekian approach of the former socialist Janos Kornai (see Kornai 2008). Authors as Alec Nove still retained that socialist features could be mixed with private enterprises and "free elections," in order to achieve more than the welfare states could give in terms of social justice, but even these moderate social democratic ideas were progressively considered as old-fashioned in a world of triumphant American neoliberalism (for an update on socialism and market reforms, see Pons and Service 2010). The decline and even the demoralization of the socialist influence over the 1990s were also thus accompanied by an underlying assumption that no more political upheavals would be done in the name of socialism. That's why Hugo Chávez's political revolution in Venezuela disconcerted the new established common sense. Maybe this would not be the case for another underdeveloped nation. But Venezuela had the biggest oil reserves in the world, and this changed everything.

2.2 Chávez's Rise

Chávez's ascension and ideas are spread throughout many types of historical sources and have already received much attention.[3] These sources include interviews, discourses, political documents, and even Chávez's books. These next two sections make a short commentary on his historical ascension as a political leader and on some of his economic ideas.

Celso Furtado did not foresee the possibility of a radical political change in Venezuela over the 1970s. Hélio Jaguaribe, another renowned Latin American intellectual, also did not predict the possibility of a historical change in Venezuela by means of an alliance between left-wing forces and the military. In light of the economic crisis of the middle 1970s, his work *Crises and Alternatives for Latin America* (Jaguaribe 1976) predicted three main historical alternatives for the region: (1) ongoing dependence and the consolidation of a so-called colonial fascism as a response to declining economic conditions; (b) the revolutionary alternative, based on Marxism-Leninism or similar "anti-imperialist" approaches; and (3) reformism conducted by some "few organized Latin American political parties" such as – allegedly – COPEI and AD in Venezuela or "radical reformism" conducted by the military, such as in Peru (Jaguaribe 1976, p.129). However, the ascension of Chávez and his political movement centered around a "socialist Bolivarianism" could be described as a mix of (2) and (3).

It is not necessary to be an *anti-Chavista* to recognize the limits and failures around Chávez administrations, as it is not necessary to be a *Chavista* to recognize his merits. As Dos Santos observed, "Chávez was an attentive reader and a voracious reader, who had the humility of learning with the books and life" (Dos Santos 2018, p.88). A more precise psychological evaluation of his character could be done not only by means of interpreting his actions as a soldier or as a politician but also by the memories of those who knew him and also by his behavior during his public

[3] For Chávez's biography, see, for example, Jones 2008, Gott 2005, Carrol 2013, Ottero 2014, Bistoletti 2011, and Mancilla 2014; for his writings and discourses, see Chávez Frías 2005, 2009, 2012, 2013 [1991], and 2013b.

appearances, especially his several interviews (for those who lived with Chávez, see Elizalde and Báez 2004). A disciplined student, *mestizo* Chávez showed great strength of character and a deep sense of social justice, which can be understood in light of his family background of school teachers and small farmers in the countryside.

Chávez's capacity to innovate in political terms helps to understand why his political project would overcome the traditional left parties in Venezuela, which still largely relied on the glossary of Marxism-Leninism. Besides being an autodidact in many scientific fields, Chávez was fitted with a good academic and military knowledge and a powerful memory. He showed contempt for dogmas, which could be seen by quotations that went from Bolívar to Marx, from Nietzsche to the Bible. His many types of intellectual references did not show superficial eclecticism, but his own sincere reflections – right or wrong – and the fact that his firm ideological conceptions were not a result of simple innate beliefs or *clichés*, but of a conscious decision. He was also a Christian, emphasizing the social aspects of this religion, arguing that Christ had been "the first socialist revolutionary."

Obviously, these features did not prevent misconceptions or eventually empty rhetoric, especially when concerning macroeconomics, a field in the social sciences which Chávez did not master so well. Until 2008, he often showed much optimism regarding the Venezuelan economy, an optimism that, as we shall see, did not entirely correspond to reality. In any case, he was not worried about dogmas and a priori conceptions. He moved around a dialectical confrontation between clear notional boundaries, such as social justice, anti-imperialism, nationalism, and tradition (as the opposite of pure imitation of foreign models), but always argued that novelty and invention should be a basic feature of any political project. "We must invent or we will get wrong" (*Inventamos o erramos*) was one of his favorite quotations from Simón Rodriguez, Bolívar's mentor.[4]

But it is obvious that Chávez did not invent alone the doctrine of a Bolivarian socialism, nor his ascension was a simple product of his inherent qualities. Venezuela had already built up a tradition of anti-imperialism that dated back to the 1800s, departing from the independence struggle coordinated by Simón Bolívar and other national revolutionaries. Venezuelan politicians and intellectuals had already made a critical reflection as regards the negative aspects of the oil industry to the Venezuelan economy; Rómulo Betancourt, for example, often mentioned and discussed the issue, declaring by 1962 that "creating new sources of wealth and thus diversifying our economy, still so dependent on oil, is a goal of capital importance" (Betancourt 2006 [1962] p.352). The Communist Party of Venezuela was founded in 1931 and constituted one important political group. As we saw, AD itself amounted a revolutionary tradition before becoming one of the ruling parties in Venezuela after 1958. "Bolivarianism," the adaptation of Marxism to Latin America (including in the intellectual legacy of José C. Mariátegui), developmentalism, and

[4] Simón Rodriguez was born in 1769 in Caracas and died in 1854, in Peru; a humanist philosopher, he was Simón Bolívar's mentor.

correlated ideas already existed when Chávez entered the military academy.[5] Under the influence of the Cuban Revolution, new revolutionary groups spread over the 1960s and 1970s, many leaving the Communist Party, which was saw as too moderate (see Löwy 1999 [ed.] and Hobsbawm 2016). Chávez maintained contact with many of those revolutionaries. And during Chávez's ascension, many other left-wing groups also disputed power, such as *MAS* (*Movimiento al Socialismo*), *La Causa R*, *Patria para Todos*, *Proyecto Carabobo*, etc. (see Bistoletti 2011).

Therefore, Chávez's trajectory performed the classic dialectical situation in history where the great individuals are both the result of past history and one important cause of historical change. Chávez's personal rise is in fact the result of a historical process, the neoliberal crisis in Venezuela by the end of the 1980s, and the loss of prestige of the ruling political groups that it entailed. He and his left-wing fellows in fact conspired against the regime since the end of the 1970s, when many oscillated between the *guerrillas* or remained as a soldier. In the end, he did not leave the army, but started to develop a so-called civilian-military alliance, seeing this strategy as a more efficient way of reaching power (see Ramonet 2016). "Like Douglas [Bravo, one of the well-known Venezuelan revolutionaries at that time], I was all for a civilian-military alliance, but I thought the seed of the movement should be sown and developed in the heart of the Army itself, from inside" (Ramonet 2016, p.528).

The plan of a military coup gained "subjective" conditions for its implementation after the *Caracazo* in 1989. As the popular manifestations were treated with a massacre by the Pérez's administration, this consolidated a psychological climate for a regime change. On 4 February 1992, the insurrection was launched; it failed, but Pérez's administration was weakened. Chávez's reputation became particularly strong when he assumed the responsibility for the operation in front of the TV cameras before being arrested, saying that: "By now, our aims were still not achieved...." José Vicente Rangel, Chávez's vice-president between 2002 and 2007, rightly observed that those images constituted a masterpiece in terms of mass politics. Chávez was imprisoned until 1994; in the meantime, he studied, met with militants and intellectuals, and reflected upon several political, historical, and economic issues. Being released during Caldera's presidency amidst great street celebrations, Chávez then left the army and decided to explore these favorable conditions by pacific means: instead of organizing another insurrection, he convinced his allies in the MBR-200, not without difficulties, that they should struggle through political means, with the creation of a "popular front." This strategy worked and the *Movimiento V República* (MVR) was born.[6] Chávez began to travel over Venezuela, always accompanied by his loyal disciple, Nicolás Maduro (born in 1962).

[5] For historical accounts of the economic and political ideas in Latin America from different theoretical perspectives, see Jaguaribe 1967, Love 1994, Sader and Jinkings 2007, and Löwy 1999.

[6] Presumably, the first Republic ranging from 1831, when Venezuela split from Gran Colombia, to the beginning of the presidency of Juan Vicente Gómez (started in 1908); Gomez's, Contrera's, and Angarita's administrations formed the second period; the coup of 1948 and the dictatorship of Pérez Jiménez that followed until 1958 constituted the Third Republic; the Fourth Republic referred to the period inaugurated by the *Punto Fijo* pact in 1958; according to Chávez and his followers, it now should be replaced by a new regime.

After those years of political mobilization between 1994 and 1998 and then a presidential campaign, Chávez was elected president in 1998. He ran against Henrique Salas Römer, representing the conservative *Projeto Venezuela* (which included members of the old COPEI). MVR's victory put an end to the traditional dispute between COPEI and AD parties, which had already been finished for practical purposes when Rafael Caldera was elected for the second time in 1994 as the candidate of a new party, the *Convergencia*, a dissidence from COPEI. In political terms, Chávez took a clear decision in 1994, when visiting Cuba after being released. However, at that moment, he did not stress socialism, but national independence and a new national constituent. His meeting with Fidel Castro in fact showed a particularly strong ideological strength in a world of triumphant neoliberalism, but Chávez did not declare to pursue socialism during his first presidential campaign. He insisted on the necessity of overcoming neoliberalism and Venezuela's problems, related to corruption, old political practices, external debt, and oil dependence. Instead of revolution, Chavez's proposed a "Bolivarian" path to Venezuela, which would begin by means of a new constitution.

2.3 The Bolivarian Project

In light of all these intellectual legacies, Chávez proposed a social doctrine centered on the Venezuelan history, in order to gather a wider support and to "nationalize" his political project. The short *El libro azul* (*The Blue Book*), written in 1991, condensed the ideas that he and his allies were discussing since the end of the 1970s in the army:

> We live, in fact, in an era when ideologies seemed to be extinguished. The 'end of ideologies', as it was called by no few academics. The phenomenon acquires greater proportions in America, particularly in Venezuela, where the great majority of the political parties, which emerged in parallel with the process of industrialization, became populist organizations, being deprived of ideological content. On the other hand, there has been a persistent tendency, among our contemporary thinkers, to seek models in other latitudes, trying to import and to implant them in our societies. Meanwhile, our people has been distancing itself more and more from its historical roots, from where they can surely find the keys to decipher the terrible puzzle that keeps us going and coming through the abyss of history, which now faces the 20th century. The ideologies are a tool of navigation to furrow [*surcar*] time and space, giving precise directions to societies and nations. (Chávez Frías 2013 [1991] p.41–42)

This book was divided in three parts: "The Tree of the Three Roots," the "Simón Bolívar National Project," and "Ideological System." The writings of Simón Bolívar, his mentor Simón Rodriguez (who subsequently changed his name to Samuel Robinson), and the "general of the sovereign people" Ezequiel Zamora[7] were

[7] Ezequiel Zamora was born in 1817 in Cúa, Venezuela, and died in 1860, in San Carlos, Venezuela. He was the leader of *Federalists* during the Federal War of 1859–1863.

condensed in the so-called Tree of the Three Roots or EBR system (Ezequiel [Zamora], [Simón] Bolívar, and [Samuel] Robinson). Bolívar was the revolutionary, Rodríguez was his intellectual mentor, and Zamora was the one who "walked by the *Llanos* invoking the betrayed Bolivarian revolution" (Chávez Frías 2013 [1991] p.91).

In light of Rodriguez's ideas, the "tree with the three roots" should be a humanist "ideological system" that followed the necessity of "inventing new institutions to the new Latin American republics [so as to avoid] the mistake of simply adopting models originated in other times, coming from other types of habits [*actitudes*], other men" (Chávez Frías 2013 [1991] p.47). The Simón Bolívar national project stressed the necessity of deepening national autonomy and popular sovereignty by means of a more democratic system of elections. The book also elaborated on Zamora's proposed type of federalism and the division of state powers between an executive branch, a legislative, a judicial, an electoral, and a *moral* one (Chávez Frías 2013 [1991] p.68). The new model for society should be based on "participation and solidarity," with "protagonistic citizens." European models for political and social organization should always be adapted to the Latin American conditions. Socialism, however, was not mentioned as such, as if the expression itself did not refer to the local realities. As regards the political organization of the state, Chávez observed: "The citizens who to belong to the different electoral councils will be total and absolutely independent from political parties" (Chávez Frías 2013 [1991] p.71), a proposal that differed from the traditional communist type of state organization, but which was unlikely to be implemented as such. Here we can see how Chávez's perspectives on foreign models of social organization would be subsequently established: he did not think that foreign models of socialism should be pursued per se. He believed instead in the necessity of creating something new for Venezuela, avoiding the alleged mistakes of mere imitation.

Another important source for Chávez's thought before reaching power was the short *And How to Scape from This Labyrinth?*" (*¿Y como salir de este laberinto?*), written in jail in 1992. Published by *El Correo Boliviariano*, MBR-200's journal, and signed by Chávez and the chief members of the organization, the document called for a new national charter, which should reunite all different members of society (Evangelical and Catholic churches, trade unions, entrepreneurs, peasants, political parties, indigenous, students, intellectuals). Andrés Pérez's resignation should be debated and implemented; then a new national constituent should be called. The ideological system such as exposed by *The Blue Book* was indirectly invoked as the intellectual foundations of this new national constituent. The "transition government" should reduce the number of ministries and eliminate the alleged "autocratic character" of the army.

The document then tackled the economic measures that should be implemented: the recall of Pérez's "economic package," measures to reduce the living costs and to foster "productive employment" and the "food sovereignty" by means of a new system of production and distribution on a national level, the adoption of self-management and supportive practices, a new tax system that allowed for lower fiscal deficits, the revision of the "letter of intents" to the IMF, and strong punishment of corruption. The members of the MBR-200 were adopting an anti-neoliberal stance, under the influence of socialist intellectuals and political leaders such as Carlos Matús, Oscar Varsavsky, and Julius Nyerere, but not socialist goals – in the sense of a broad socialization of the economy and the adoption of some kind of central planning. Socialism was not yet the goal at the beginning of the 2000s, and the word as such would not be mentioned in the presidential discourses until 2003 (see Chávez Frías 2013b, vols. I–II):

> [By 1991] we hadn't yet raised the flag of socialism. At the same time, we were always inclined that way. We looked to Cuba and Nicaragua as local examples, and, further away, to the Soviet Union as a potential ally. The defeat of Daniel Ortega's government hit us hard… Of course, the strength of our own movement, militarily speaking, lay in Bolivarianism. Our military, revolutionary, insurgent organization was not affected in itself by those international events. But in political terms, we were obviously affected by that 'end of socialism' atmosphere. Particularly considering the direction we wanted our new Venezuela foreign policy to take, looking for new horizons…. (see Ramonet 2016, p.755)

In fact, the abovementioned documents contained the political and economic guidelines of Chávez's first presidential campaign in 1998. They criticized the ruling political groups in Venezuela, the social inequality, the unemployment, and the IMF and neoliberalism, but not capitalism per se. Dependence, imperialism, monopolies, and unequal distribution were the main targets. These ideas were merged into the first general guidelines of the economic policies contained in the document *Plan Nación 2001–2007*, written in 2001 still under a relatively conservative tone (see República Bolivariana de Venezuela [RBV] 2001). It showed a mix of heterodox and orthodox approaches, showing even some neoliberal perspectives, as the autonomy for the Central Bank and the maintenance of a floating exchange rate regime. In general terms, the plan expressed generic neo-developmentalist ideas, showing Chávez's initial cautious positions, and also the political climate prevailing until 2002. Through the *Fondo Para el Desarrollo Social* (FONDEN, created in 2005), the government intended to use the surplus resources provided by PDVSA (Petróleos de Venezuela S.A., the largest state-owned oil enterprise) to improve fiscal conditions during downturns and to diversify oil resources into other forms of investments.[8] Autonomy, endogenous growth, industrialization, import substitution,

[8] In other terms, diversifying the economic structure, reaching a sustainable economic growth, removing severe economic volatility, refining oil and developing the domestic production of machinery and technology, developing the "social economy," reaching fiscal balances and higher saving and investment rates, reinforcing the small-scale and cooperative enterprises and the domestic production of food, reinforcing institutional conditions, and developing the domestic financial markets (see República Bolivariana de Venezuela 2001 and also Campbell and Cömert 2009). The rate of exchange between the sales of PDVSA's hard currencies and the Central Bank would be determined according to the context, not being tied to any of the existing rates of exchange. According to the PDVSA, the Exchange Agreement Number 35 "sets forth the rules that will govern the operations of the foreign currency exchange control regime fixing the protected exchange rate (*DIPRO for its Spanish acronym*) at Bs.9.98 per dollar for purchases and per dollar for sales at their effective date price. Such exchange agreement also indicates the activities to which each type of exchange rate corresponds. Foreign currencies purchase and sale transactions generated by export and/or sale operations of PDVSA and its subsidiaries hydrocarbons activities, as well as those of the Empresas Mixtas referred to in the Organic Hydrocarbons Law, the Organic

diversification, etc. appeared as the leading goals to achieve, following the ideas of the Economic Commission for Latin America and the Caribbean, including those of Osvaldo Sunkel.

Chávez decided to "raise the flag of socialism" after the political and economic difficulties of 2002–2003, which involved a coup against him, his kidnapping, and the strikes in PDVSA. After returning to power, a clear decision was made to reinforce his popular support through a new political appeal. Chávez started to sincerely believe in it, beginning at the same time to use the power of socialist ideas to mobilize society and particularly the poor. This should be the "socialism for the XXI century," suggesting that the "old" one should be surpassed. In theoretical terms, this was a legitimate and interesting instance, but it also implied that the lessons of history and economic theory may also have been ignored. By claiming a new socialism, Chávez was both trying to avoid the general disappointment born from the Soviet history and also trying to develop a political project around the Venezuelan historical features. This "new" socialism should be based on the constant mobilization of the civil society, progressive legislation, free public services, as well as the fostering not only of state firms but also of cooperatives, "social production companies," and land reform; politically, it should be based on democratic means, a place for the "market" being assured, including private enterprises (for a discussion, see Azzellini 2009). An immediate removal of private enterprises as such should be avoided; oil dependence, imperialism, and monopoly were the fundamental economic problems to be faced. Only the unproductive fractions of the bourgeoisie should be attacked. No mentions to physical targets and an overall coordinating plan which linked the central government and the "comunas" (*communes*) were mentioned; socialism should exclude forced means to capital accumulation, being born basically from local ("communal") participatory decisions.

Accordingly, the economic guidelines of the economy after 2003 were based on these news assumptions (its economic aspects will be analyzed in the next chapter). The intellectual aspects of this new ideological and political stage can be tracked from many sources, including the type of literature that Chávez read and used to mention (Kenneth Galbraith, Noam Chomsky, Istvan Mészáros, etc.), but mainly from his own words. These were condensed with more clarity in the so-called "Red Book" (*El Libro Rojo*), the statute of the new Unified Socialist Party of Venezuela (*Partido Socialista Unificado de Venezuela* (PSUV)) created in 2007. Chávez was its president. Most of the previous political organizations under Chávez's political

---

Law on Gaseous Hydrocarbons and the Organic Law for the Development of Petrochemical Activities will be completed at any of the exchange rates provided for in this exchange agreement (reduced in 0.25% for sales), taking into account the programming, coordination and assessments made by the Sectoral Vice Presidency of the Economy, the Ministry of People's Power for Banking and Finance, and the BCV, on the basis of the policies established and the availability of foreign currencies to meet the economy's needs, governed by the exchange rate referred to in this agreement" (Petróleos de Venezuela [PDVSA] 2016, p.74).

influence, as the *Movimiento V República* (MVR), the *Unidad Popular Venezolana* (Venezuelan Popular Unity), the *Liga Socialista* (Socialist League), the Tupamaro Movement, and other left-wing groups, would all be merged into the new PSUV (the Communist Party remaining outside).

The PSUV assumed itself like a socialist party struggling for a socialist Venezuela which still did not exist. It stressed the perils of contemporary imperialism and the need for an ecological interpretation of the economic growth. The majority of the essential means of production should be nationalized. Tactical and strategic alliances could eventually be made with "other forces" in the "struggle for socialism" (PSUV 2010, p.85). "Bourgeois" democracy should give place to "participatory and protagonistic democracy." Corruption and bureaucratization should be fought; oil dependence and consumerism should give place to economic diversification and the "full satisfaction of the human needs" (PSUV 2010, p.43). Agriculture should also be fostered, as well as the balance between export-driven growth and endogenous growth (PSUV 2010, p.125–126). The party apparently made a self-criticism when observing that during the first years of the now so-called Bolivarian Revolutionary Government, "it was given priority to the social inclusion [which] demanded fast and massive responses"; it apparently meant that according to the party, the government did not give priority to a fast rate of investments. The *misiones* (government social policies centered on a local level [communal councils]) were created as a means to "overcome the bureaucratic and heavy structure of the old bourgeois state by means of the oil rents" (PSUV 2010, p.28). It was now time (2007) to struggle for a socialist Venezuela (p.29), which should be built from the bottom upward, by means of more *comunas* (communes), local councils (*consejos comunales*), and "revolutionary councils of workers and students" (p.33).

As it can be seen, the founders of the PSUV were apparently trying to recover aspects of the original Soviet structures that led to the revolution of 1917; but despite some brief mentions to economic planning (see PSUV 2010, p.32, p.108, and p.130), they apparently ignored the historical vicissitudes of building the Soviet state and its equivalents in Eastern Europe and Asia. Excluding Mao and Guevara (for a few years), most of the historical figures quoted by PSUV's statute did not participate in the construction of the so-called "real existing socialism," with their centralized states and practical problems to be solved. In fact these postrevolutionary states were not taken as "socialist states," and their related functioning did not deserve close attention, including Tito's Yugoslavia, which should have been an obvious reference to Chávez and the PSUV not only because that former nation inaugurated the discussion of the market socialism and self-managed enterprises in a socialist economy but also because of its role in the "nonaligned" movement to which Venezuela also belonged to. The founders of PSUV did not mention the main socialist thinkers of the economics of socialism, as well-known Oskar Lange, Michal Kalecki, Leonid Kantorovich, etc.; Western critics such as Ernst Mandel or Alec Nove were not mentioned as well (for Mandel's perspectives on the Soviet economy, see Mandel 1962, Chapters 15–17; see also Nove 1992). Surprisingly,

Marx, who never mentioned the concrete functioning of a socialist economy, was taken as the main theoretical reference in terms of economic policies. "It is necessary to take the theoretical instruments of the critique of the political economy such as elaborated by Marx and Marxist authors to elaborate a critique of political economy for the [socialist] transition which give solutions [not only] to general but also to immediate and concrete problems" (PSUV 2010, p.117):

> The Party will struggle to train its militants with the [ideology] of the Tree of the three roots -the thought and actions of Simón Bolívar, Simón Rodriguez and Ezequiel Zamora- and will recover [*rescatará*] with critical sense the historical experiences of socialism, adapting as a guide the thought and the actions of Latin American and world revolutionaries and socialists such as José Martí, Ernesto Che Guevara, José Carlos Mariátegui, Rosa Luxemburg, Karl Marx, Friedrich Engels, Lenin, Trotsky, Gramsci, Mao Tse-Tung and other who contributed to the struggle for a world of equality and social justice, a human experience which has far antecedents, such as the Afro-Indian worldviews [*cosmovisión*], Christianity [and] the Theology of Liberation. (PSUV 2010, p.38)

It is true that the party adopted many Leninist features. It declared having an "eternal leader" – Hugo Chávez – and to represent the interests of the "urban and rural proletariat and other exploited sectors" on the basis of the democratic centralism (p.53). Militants had a list of obligations, centered on a socialist *ethos*. A new V Socialist International should be organized (p.95). But the so-called comuna (communal council) should be the base of the new society and the socialist state. Several types of property could exist, but the majority of the means of production should not belong to private individuals or large private corporations; private property should have a "social function" (*función social*). The government should foster state enterprises, including their eventual associations with foreign companies. But state enterprises should be progressively transferred to the *consejos comunales*, that is, communal councils (PSUV 2010, p.119). Here, the proposed model had an obvious historical preceding, which was the Yugoslavian type of socialism; Chávez and the PSUV, however, did not take it for granted, the Cuban case being their favorite reference, though not completely (for a discussion, see Yaffe 2015).

2.4 An Appreciation

One interesting thing about Chávez and the then so-called Movimiento V República itself is that unlike other progressive leaders and parties after the fall of the Berlin Wall, they did not reject a socialist project as such. It was as if Venezuela's left forces were almost autonomous with regard to the world events after 1989 (as Chávez told Ramonet; see Ramonet 2016). By means of personal readings and also academic studies, Chávez came to know the shortcomings of the Soviet political and economic model and decided to overcome them, although retaining the socialist *appeal* for equality and national sovereignty so common in Africa and Asia over the last century. Accordingly, he personally did not propose a complete socialization of the means of production in Venezuela in 1998, and did not seem to propose it even after 2003, despite the PSUV's statements on these matters. He still thought that being Venezuela a poor nation, productive private capitals – including foreign ones – were still necessary even in socialism (for a discussion, see Mancilla 2014).

Initially, Chávez planned a radicalization of the bourgeois democracy or something more than that, also without pursuing a complete monopoly of the political power for his party. This model assumed a permanent political tension. Theoretically, his supporters would have to live side by side with the opposition – conservative, virulent, diversified (there are more than 90 political parties in Venezuela today). Beyond Chávez's original and sincere beliefs in democracy as an apparent "universal value," there was in fact no other way to behave by 1998, given the number of opposing political groups in the nation and the international mood against communist perspectives over the 1990s. Thus Chávez firstly proposed a political model based on a permanent struggle, on his *charisma* among the people and the army, and on concrete actions toward the poor people: "the bourgeoisie and their allies -at home and abroad- will never leave us in peace. And that's normal in democratic rivalry. We have to get used, therefore, to living in a state of permanent struggle, in permanent conflict, in permanent revolution" (see Ramonet 2016, p.976).[9]

There is no reason to suppose that this statement was not sincere, but as time passed, Chávez evidently took advantage from the fact that the party was growing in popular support in order to accept more or less free elections, also taking covered measures to reinforce his power, as reforming the Armed Forces and creating a popular *militia*. This path avoided political apathy and foreign criticism, which were also important in a world of fierce opposition to any type of radical economic and social policies. From the point of view of state planning and the monopoly of the political power by the ruling socialist party, this would reveal itself a dangerous game, as the opposition tried a coup, won some elections, governed regional administrations, and maintained an open attack through different means. The turn to a socialist project apparently reduced Chávez's beliefs or public defense of (liberal) democracy, but he professed the need for elections until the end.

Anyway, the dangers brought by the coup in 2002 led to Chávez's political change toward socialism. But this socialism was not based on the Soviet or the Chinese economic models. Chávez took for granted that those models were not real socialism, dismissing their historical achievements and particularly the economic theory and techniques behind economic planning. In order to avoid "bureaucratization," state property should be transferred to local producers, but – interestingly enough – no reference to the Yugoslavian model of self-management was made, as if the new "Bolivarian" model should start without historical references. The

[9] For positive or balanced discussions of Chávez's rise and social policies, see Harnecker 2005 and Guevara 2005 (interviews with Chávez); Clairmont 2007; Bruce 2008; Jones 2008; Martinez et al. 2010; Gonzalez 2014; Cicariello-Maher 2016; and Strønen 2017; for typical critiques based on the pejorative notions of "populism," see Hawkins 2010; for a Laclausian interpretation of Chávez "populism," see Brading 2013; for other critiques, see also Dos Santos 2016 and 2019 and Sutherland 2018.

original Yugoslavian perspectives of fighting hierarchy and absent property in work places could have been taken as a point of departure; there was plenty of literature on this issue (see, for example, Adizes 1977). Of course no one could deny that the Soviet model should be reevaluated and interpreted in historical perspective. But proposals made on this stance had already been tested elsewhere, and it was seen that it also had problems. It would have been very useful to turn to these past experiences before putting so much trust in self-management, decentralization, and even the domestic bourgeoisie, which could not be simply taken as magic tools for overcoming the problems of the economic planning which the economic policies still declared to pursue.

As regards the system of self-managed enterprises in Yugoslavia, Brus observed:

> The process of implementation of these ideas [market socialism and self-management] was gradual and by no means straightforward. The problem of de-controlling prices and foreign economic relations, both essential for creating competitive conditions, proved to be particularly difficult. [...] Empirical evidence suggests that the attempt to combine market mechanism with self-management of the Yugoslavian kind generate problems unknown either to capitalist market economy or to full-fledged cooperatives operating in a market environment. Decentralization of state functions substantially enhanced the power of local organizations (particularly at level of national republics and autonomous regions) which led to strong autarkic tendencies that not only had a disruptive effect on the unity of national market, but also made easier to overrule the commercial principles of operation (e.g. of the banks) by political-administrative interference. [...] Excessive fragmentation resulted in some cases. [...] [T]he end of the 1970s and the beginning of the 1980s brought substantial deterioration in this respect (slowdown of growth, high unemployment, accelerated inflation, fall in real earnings), which prompted renewed scrutiny of the effectiveness of the Yugoslavian model. (Brus 1990, p.169–171)

Reflecting on the writings on "bureaucratization" made by left-wing economists, Alec Nove was also skeptical regarding many aspects of those critiques:

> It cannot be too strongly emphasised that complexity is not just a quantitative matter: as Marxists should know, quantity passes into quality. Such vital questions as decentralisation and centralisation, plan and market, the interests of the part and the interests of the whole, the identification of the public good, the alienation of individuals, the necessity and dangers of hierarchy and bureaucracy and, incidentally, most of the major problems now plaguing the Soviet economy, all arise directly or indirectly out of the *vast scale and innumerable interdependencies* of the modern industrial economy. It will not and cannot be 'simple'. The economy cannot be planned and run 'like the post office'. It is not just a matter of technique plus accounting-arithmetic, as Lenin (before 1918) seemed naively to imagine. [...] Then some other departments (numerous different departments, because of the scale of the task) have to ensure that the means are available, or can be produced, or provided from stock. Even the most 'motivated' worker, manager, or production-planning department cannot ensure that action is taken unless the means are provided, and the means (i.e. the various inputs) are bound to be administered by several other departments. Hence the *paperasserie*, interdepartmental conferences, regulations, delays, inconsistencies, the need to refer questions to higher authority, and other well-known examples of bureaucracy. To denounce it is easy, but it has its vital role in production in a centrally planned marketless economy, and so it grows and 'flourishes.' (Nove 1992, p.33–35)

In the case of the Soviet model of economic planning, Chávez frequently repeated some of these well-known commonplaces, though he also seemed to understand that the problems of a socialist economy were very complex and should be put in historical context. "Lets remember the Soviet Union, which is gone with the wind. There was never democracy in the Soviet Union, never socialism; their leaders have never realized, or they could not do anything"; however, the "guilty also comes from the external aggressions, economic sabotages, biological wars" made by the "Empire" (the United States) (Chávez Frías 2012, p.16). As regards the case of the Chinese model after Deng Xiaoping, which maintained a decisive role for state control even after the adoption of market reforms,[10] Chávez simply did not talk about it. China mattered as an important trade partner or geopolitical ally; but apparently Chávez also did not care about the concrete functioning of the hybrid Chinese economic structure, maybe because he thought China was too far and too different (for Chávez's references on China and his silence regarding the Chinese economic model, see Chávez's Frías 2013b, vols. II–III):[11]

> A productive system that aims to activate the full participation of the associated producers, the workers, requires a multiplicity of 'parallel' processors, coordinated in the appropriate way, as well as a corresponding operating system that is radically different from the central planning alternative, be it the capitalist-led economy or its well-known post-capitalist varieties misleadingly presented as 'planning.' (Chávez Frías 2012, p.24)

The idea that "socialism is an invention" and that no "one knew how to build it," which Chávez repeatedly stated, referred to a real dilemma. Capitalism did not work well, particularly under underdeveloped features, but the Soviet model had many problems.[12] On the other hand, social democracy or traditional parties did not serve as an efficient tool of political mobilization. Socialism having been chosen, statements regarding its history were often made with more or less superficial statements. Chávez and PSUV's ideas on socialism were placed between the defense of the accumulated experiences of the past and the need of new routes in a rapidly evolving world. But this position, which was anchored on many innocent prejudices as regards the Soviet Union and the old socialist camp, often led to disdaining past experience, wasting valuable and useful knowledge that could be *adapted* to the Venezuelan conditions.

This stance led to contradictions. When Chávez claimed that "we should not continue opening factories that are like an island, surrounded by the sea of capitalism,

---

[10] "In China and Vietnam a crucial aspect of socialist planning -the political dictatorship- was retained after socialist planning as a whole was jettisoned, and this (combined with major policy and systemic changes) enabled them to experience rapid economic growth" (Ellman 2014, p.20).

[11] During an interview to the Argentinean public service broadcaster *Canal 7*, Chávez was asked by Daniel Filmus, Argentinian politician, what socialism was. He replied: "It is what is written in the books of Marx and Lenin!." But no references were made to – say – Mao, Tito, or Deng. It can be seen here the influence of Trotsky's works on Chávez's perspectives.

[12] In Ellman's words, "Marx and Engels were right to argue that an unregulated market economy was socially undesirable, but wrong to assume that the replacement of the market by planning would lead to an attractive economic and social system. Stalin was right to stress the need for backward countries to catch up, but he and his followers were wrong in thinking that the system he created would enable the countries which adopted it to catch up with the advanced countries in the civilian sector" (Ellman 2014, p.20).

because the sea swallows it up" (Chávez Frías 2012, p.27), he should have concluded that self-management and local participation should have been balanced with some kind of centralized decisions and forced accumulation decisions taken by the center. In fact, "the process of planning and counter-planning involves a mutual submission and discussion of planning suggestions, designed to lead to the adoption of a plan which is feasible for the enterprise and ensures that the resources of each enterprise are used in accordance with national requirements" (Robinson and Eatwell 1973, p.282); but how to assure these *national requirements* if decisions are being made by local producers irrespective of the central government, with firms "appropriating their own economic surplus"[13]? It is clear that by allowing the domestic enterprises to manage their own resources meant a smaller degree of economic control of the economy as whole – control which is needed to overcome underdevelopment by means of a strong accumulation of capital. This is even more difficult if, instead of public, nationalized or "social production enterprises," the private firms still prevails in terms of the GDP.

PSUV's statute and the government subsequent "socialist plans" since 2003 were full of moral indignation and general trends to be achieved, but they did not mention more specific techniques historically related to socialist policies. This stance is connected with the limited economic policies adopted over the period and may be taken at least as a partial reason for the unbalanced behavior of the economy. The point here is not that self-management should not have been adopted. The question is that both in the case of a new "communal state" without a full central planning or – more realistically – a hybrid economy where self-managed enterprises constituted only a share of the total firms and private capitals played a decisive role (such as in China after Deng), the public and private sectors of the economy should have been stimulated by the implementation of *macroeconomic decisions* that assured them aggregate demand and extensive accumulation. This would involve high saving rates, lower consumption rates, and devaluated exchange rates in order to boost domestic manufacturing (including tradable goods), in parallel with stronger measures to boost agriculture. This would also involve higher rates of interest for unproductive consumption, a much stronger stance on private speculation and hoarding, strict limits to capital export, etc. However, as we shall see, despite the official commitment to these goals and many concrete actions toward them, the economy saw a growing propensity to import and stagnated and then downward rates of investment in terms of the GDP, particularly in the manufacturing sectors, low or falling rates of agricultural production on a per capita basis, negative real interest rates connected with an overvalued domestic currency, speculation spread rapidly, and the lowering of real wages boosted the share of profits in the GDP without being used as an addition source of savings by the government, particularly after 2013. Even in the case of a full socialist economy of self-managed enterprises – which was far from the case – the decisions to correct all these correlated trends

[13]As established by the economic guidelines of the government, see RBV 2007 and Chap. 3.

could not be made by local producers; it was the task of the central government, of its economic policy.

In any case, the conceptions around the role of self-managed firms were only a part of the events; the private sector of the economy remained dominant in terms of the GDP (70% of the economy by 2017; see Sect. 4.2). In light of that, the adopted economic policies remained largely linked to the capitalist sectors of the economy, which, according to the government, should have a role even in socialism. Many of the adopted policies were correct in developmental terms, such as the new legislation regarding agriculture, but they lacked a firm commitment to domestic industrial growth.

Economic policies were, by its turn, only a part of the complex history involving the so-called Bolivarian period. It should be stressed that the type of economic growth that Venezuela showed since 1999 could have persisted over a larger period without so huge crises in the oil markets (the first impacts of the 2008 crisis,[14] the competition coming from the shale gas and related technologies in the United States, then the downward trend for prices, and finally American sanctions, particularly after 2017). Without a radical change in oil markets, economic policies could have been eventually improved toward import substitution under more calm conditions. At the same time, Venezuela faced the fierce domestic opposition of private groups, regardless of the soft stance of the government toward many between them (for a discussion, see Ellner 2017). Thus, the macroeconomic policies adopted by the government should be taken into account in the evaluation of the shortcomings of the Venezuelan economy over the period, but historical analysis should consider all these variables in a broad evaluation.

[14] "The outbreak of the Global Financial Crisis (GFC), which originated in the United States and reached its trough in late 2008 and early 2009, changed [the] situation dramatically. The increased commercial and financial openness that most developing countries had embraced during the reforms of the 1990s in the successful pursuit of improved efficiency and growth had as its flip side heightened exposure to external real and financial shocks, and the shocks of both types generated by the GFC proved to be severe indeed. Once again, international turbulence aggravated the stabilization challenge for developing countries, and once again stabilization issues moved to center stage. Issues such as the appropriate management of the domestic financial system, policy responses to capital inflows and outflows, the formulation of exchange-rate policy, and the pursuit of monetary and fiscal policy regimes that simultaneously achieve medium-term credibility and short-run flexibility, have once again moved to the center of the policy debate. As in the past, these issues have emerged in distinctive form among developing countries, where greater commercial openness, more fickle capital flows, less well-established macroeconomic institutions and policy regimes, and significantly less confidence in macroeconomic management have all combined to produce especially acute challenges" (Agénor and Montiel 2018, p. xix).

References

Adizes I (1977) Autogestión: la práctica yugoslava. Mexico City, Fondo de Cultura Económica

Agénor PR, Montiel PJ (2018) Development macroeconomics, 4th edn. Princeton University Pres, Princeton

Azzellini D (2009) Venezuela's solidarity economy: collective ownership, expropriation, and workers' self-management. WorkingUSA J Labor Soc 12:171–1971

Barbosa WN (2017) One hundred years of learning: The Russian Revolution of 1917. Agrarian South 6(2):221–236

Betancourt R (2006) Selección de escritos políticos (1929–1981). Caracas, Fundación Rómulo Betancourt

Bistoletti EL (2011) Estudio sobre los orígines del Chavismo. Editorial Académica Española, Madrid

Brading R (2013) Populism in Venezuela. Routledge, London

Brown A (2009) The rise and fall of communism. Harper-Collins, New York

Bruce I (2008) The real Venezuela. Pluto Press, Norwich

Brus W (1973) The economics and politics of socialism, collected essays. Routledge, London

Brus W (1990) Market socialism. In: Eatwell J, Milgate M, Newman P (eds) Problems of the planned economy. Macmillan, London

Campbell A, Cömert H (2009) Progressive Third World Central Banking and the case of Venezuela. In: Saad-Filho, A and Yalman, G (eds). Economic transitions to neoliberalism in Middle-income countries. London, Routledge

Carrol R (2013) Comandante, Hugo Chávez's Venezuela. Penguin Press, London

Chávez Frías H (2005) Selección de discursos del Presidente de la República Bolivariana de Venezuela, vol 1–8. Caracas, Ediciones de la Presidencia de la República

Chavez Frías H (2009) Introduction'. In: Brown M (ed) The Bolivarian revolution. Verso, London

Chavez Frías H (2012) Golpe de Timón. I Consejo de Ministros del nuevo ciclo de la Revolución Bolivariana. Ediciones Correo del Orinoco, Caracas

Chávez Frías H (2013 [1991]) El Libro Azul. Gobierno de Venezuela, Caracas

Chávez Frías H (2013b) Discursos del Presidente ante la Asamblea Nacional (1999–2012), vol I–IV. Feditorial de la Assemblea Nacional William Lara, Caracas

Chávez Frías H et al (1992) Una propuesta. ¿Y como salir de este labirinto? In: El Correo Bo- liviariano. Movimiento Revolucionário – 200. Available on https://dolartoday.com/este-es-el-documento-original-de-chavez-llamando-la-transicion-firmas/

Cicariello-Maher G (2016) Building the commune. Radical democracy in Venezuela. Verso, London

Clairmont F (2007) Cuba and Venezuela, the nemeses of imperialism. Malaysia, Citizens International

Dos Santos FL (2016) A crise da esquerda brasileira em perspectiva latino-americana. São Paulo, Editora Elefante

Dos Santos FL (2018) Uma história da onda progressista Sul-Americana (1998–2016). São Paulo, Editora Elefante

Dos Santos FL (2019) Power and impotence. A history of South America under progressivism (1998–2016). Brill, Leiden

Eatwell J, Milgate M, Newman P (eds) (1990) Problems of the planned economy. Macmillan, London

Elizalde RM, Báez L (2004) Chávez nuestro. Casa Editora Abril, La Habana

Ellman M (2014) Socialist planning. Cambridge University Press, Cambridge

Ellman M, Kontorovich, V (1992) The disintegration of the Soviet System. London, Routledge

Ellner S (2017) Venezuela's fragile revolution. From Chávez Maduro Month Rev 69(5)

Fürst J, Pons S, Selden M (eds) (2017) The Cambridge history of communism, vol III. Cambridge University Press, Cambridge, UK

Furtado C (1977) Economic development of Latin America. Cambridge Economic Press, Cambridge, UK
Gonzalez M (2014) Hugo Chávez, socialist for the twenty-first century. Pluto Press, Ewards Bros
Gott R (2005) Hugo Chávez and the Bolivarian revolution. Verso, London
Guevara A (2005) Chávez, Venezuela and the new Latin America, an interview with Hugo Chávez by Aleida Guevara. Ocean Press, New York
Harnecker M (2005) Understanding the Venezuelan revolution. Hugo Chávez talks to Marta Harnecker. Monthly Review, New York
Hawkins K (2010) Venezuela's Chavismo and populism in comparative perspective. Cambridge University Press, Cambridge
Hobsbawm E (1994) The age of extremes. Penguin Books, London
Hobsbawm E (2016) Viva la Revolución, Hobsbawm on Latin America. Little Brown, London
Jaguaribe H (1967) Problemas do desenvolvimento latino-americano. Civilização Brasileira, Rio de Janeiro
Jaguaribe H (1976) Crises e alternativas da América Latina. Perspectiva, São Paulo
Jones B (2008) ¡Hugo! The Hugo Chávez story from mud hut to perpetual revolution. Steerforth Press, New Hampshire
Kantorovich L (1965) The best use of economic resources. Pergamon Press, Oxford
Kornai Y (2008) From socialism to capitalism. CEU Press, Budapest
Lange O (1936) On the economic theory of socialism, part 1. Rev Econ Stud 4(1):53–71
Laski K, Brus W (1991) From Marx to market. Socialism in search of an economic system. Oxford University Press, Oxford
Love J (1994) Economic ideas and ideologies in Latin America since 1930. In: Bethell L (ed) The Cambridge history of Latin America, vol VIII. Cambridge University Press, Cambridge, UK
Löwy M (1999) O marxismo na América Latina. São Paulo, Perseu Abramo
Mandel E (1962) Traité d'économie marxiste, tome 2. Paris, René Juliard
Mancilla AS (2014) El pensamiento económico de Hugo Chávez. Quito, Instituto de Altos Estudios Nacionales
Martinez C, Fox M, Farrel J (eds) (2010) Venezuela speaks! Voices from the grassroots. PM Press, Oakland
Mazower M (1999) Dark continent. Penguin Books, London
Nove A (1992) The economics of feasible socialism. Harper-Collins, London
Nove A, Nuti DM (1972) Socialist economics. Penguin Books, London
Ottero GS (2014) Hugo Chávez y la ressucción de un pueblo. Instituto Cubano del Libro, La Habana
Partido Socialista de Venezuela Unificado (PSUV) (2010) El Libro Rojo. Documentos fundamentales, Caracas
Petróleos de Venezuela SA (2016) Consolidated financial statements. PDVSA, Caracas. Available on http://www.pdvsa.com
Piketty T (2019) Capital et ideologie. Seuil, Les Livres du Nouveau Monde
Pons S and Service R (eds) (2010) A dictionary of 20th-century communism. Princeton, Princeton University Press
Ramonet I Hugo Chávez (2016) My first life, conversations with Hugo Chávez. Verso, London
República Bolivariana de Venezuela (2001) Plan Nación 2001–2007. Gazeta Oficial de la República, Caracas. Available on http://www.mppp.gob.ve/
Robinson J, Eatwell J (1973) An introduction to modern economics. Macgraw-Hill, London
Sader E, Jinkings I (eds) (2007) Enciclopédia Contemporânea da América Latina e do Caribe. Boitempo, São Paulo
Strønen IA (2017) Grassroots politics and oil culture in Venezuela, the revolutionary petro- state. Palgrave Macmillan, London
Sutherland M (2018) La ruína de Venezuela no se deve al 'socialismo' ni a la 'revolución'. Nueva Sociedad 274
Tomba L (2010) Socialist market economy. In: Pons S, Service R (eds) A dictionary of 20th- century communism. Princeton, Princeton University Press

Wilczynski J (1972) Socialist economic development and reforms. Palgrave Macmillan, London
Wilczynski J (1981) An Encyclopedic dictionary of Marxism, socialism and communism. Macmillan Reference Books, London
Yaffe H (2015) Venezuela: building a socialist communal economy? International Critical Thought 5(1):23–41

Chapter 3
Economic Policies (1999–2018)

3.1 Introduction

This chapter summarizes in a chronological fashion the economic policies in Venezuela between 1999, when Chávez's first administration began, and 2018, when Chávez's successor Nicholas Maduro completed his first term as the new president of Venezuela. The chapter describes the evolution of economic policies in the nation over this period, which began as a mix of developmental policies and evolved to self-declared socialist goals. The chapter relies on the official data and official documents and intends to summarize the institutional, social, and political environment in Venezuela between 1999 and 2018, as a precondition to the analysis of the Venezuelan economic performance, which will be made in the next chapter.

3.2 Policies Between 1999 and 2002

The alleged conditions of a "vibrant democracy" during the *Pacto del Punto Fijo* between 1958 and 1998 are an ideological myth.[1] Venezuelan was an underdeveloped nation and had huge social problems by the end of the 1990s, particularly

[1] "On March 5, 2013, Venezuela's president Hugo Chávez died after a two-year struggle with cancer, putting an end to 14 years in the presidency. Several books have already been published over the past few years trying to assess Chávez's legacy, and many more will certainly come. This [book] is not one of them. Rather, [our] book is about Venezuela before Chávez came to power. It tries to understand how one of the continent's most prosperous nations, which boasted a vibrant democracy at a time when much of the region was mired in authoritarianism, saw a prolonged collapse of its economic and political institutions over the last two decades of the twentieth century" (Hausmann and Rodríguez 2014, p.vii). Felicien, Schiavoni, and Romero observed that "[t]he predominant narratives routinely fail to mention that at the start of the Bolivarian Revolution, more than half of the population was living in poverty, with hunger levels higher than those of today. (...)

© The Editor(s) (if applicable) and The Author(s), under exclusive license to Springer Nature Switzerland AG 2020

V. E. Schincariol, *Society and Economy in Venezuela*, SpringerBriefs in Sociology, https://doi.org/10.1007/978-3-030-60083-9_3

poverty and violence.[2] Accordingly, Chávez administrations created a flow of progressive social and economic policies which translated, in reality, the very existence of those social problems; it could not be denied that these policies were a landmark in terms of social and economic rights in Venezuela.

In political terms, the first structural change introduced by Chávez was the election of a new constituent assembly, such as promised during the electoral campaign. The new constitution of 1999 contained popular instruments of decision, incentives for cooperative production, comprehensive labor rights, and interventionist features. The text did not mention socialism, but many concrete actions were taken in order to create the political conditions for deep social, economic, and even regional changes.[3] One of the first and most important measures contained in it was the (re) nationalization of PDVSA: Article 303 established that "for reasons of economic, political and strategic national sovereignty, the state will retain the entirety of the shares of Petróleos de Venezuela S.A., or the eventual authorized organization [*ente*] of the oil industry, with the exception of its branches, strategic partnerships, enterprises and any other which may be constituted as a consequence of its business developments" (RBV 1999). As Venezuela had 302 billion barrels of proved oil reserves by that time, "the largest in the world" (IEA 2019, p.02), most of them located in the Orinoco Belt (central part of the nation), this fact alone could be regarded as one of the most brave and nationalistic measures in the history of the so-called developing nations, a fact usually not properly understood.

Under the aegis of the new constitution, Chávez was reelected for the first time in 2000, with of 59% of the total valid votes, inaugurating the so-called Fifth Republic (*V República*); Francisco Cardenas (running for the formerly radical but now moderate *La Causa R*) obtained 37%. The opposition was temporarily paralyzed, and the other left-wing groups were envious of Chávez's successes. Regional alliances were started in Latin America and the Caribbean so as to fight American interventionism and influence, such as the oil alliance *Petrocaribe* (preferential payment for oil purchases) and the intergovernmental organization *Alianza Bolivariana para los Pueblos de Nuestra América* (ALBA). Venezuela also began a closer collaboration with Cuba, exchanging medical assistance and trade for cheap oil. The

---

[A]ccording to the United Nations Food and Agriculture Organization (FAO), an average of 4.9 million people in Venezuela were undernourished each year from 1998 to 2000 (representing a fifth of the 2000 population of 24.5 million), and an average of 4.1 million from 2014–16, at the height of the shortages (13 percent of a total population of 31.5 million in 2016)" (Felicien, Schiavoni and Romero 2018, p.5 and footnote 2).

[2] "When Chávez reached power [the hypertrophy of an indiscriminate contractor state in all good periods for oil markets] was not sufficient to provide any relevant service or guarantees to the population" (Zahonero 2017, p.96).

[3] These actions involved many anti-poverty and social welfare programs, such as the well-known *Mission Vuelvan Caras*, *Missión Robinson*, and *Missión Barrio Adentro*; a new land legislation, which pointed toward a land reform and ecological and sustainable practices; new rights regarding indigenous and black people, such as the mandatory use of indigenous languages in all national schools, as well as the prohibition of fee charges; and many other progressive measures (for a detailed account of Chávez policies, see República Bolivariana de Venezuela 2019).

year of 2001 was very important in institutional terms. Being given new constitutional powers by the new national constituent, Chávez created by decrees the Investment Fund for Macroeconomic Stabilization (*Fondo de Inversión para Estabilización Macroeconómica*), which should use reserves from oil resources so as to stabilize the economy during cyclical fluctuations. The government created a new legislation regulating the extraction of fossil fuels in the economy (*Ley Orgánica de Hidrocarburos*), subsequently approved by the Congress (RBV 2006). It secured the public property of all oil reserves and stated that these resources should be used to develop the economy and to finance the wealth and education systems (Article 5); foreign and private participations in oil extraction were not forbidden, but taxes were raised, and the state control over the functioning of this industry was reassured.

There was also the introduction of new legislation for land and agricultural development (*Decreto con fuerza de ley de tierras y desarrollo agrario*, RBV [República Bolivarian de Venezuela] 2001b), which aimed at "establishing the bases of integral and sustainable rural development; [this] understood here as the fundamental means for human development and economic growth of the agrarian sector under a fair distribution of wealth and a strategic, democratic and participatory planning, eliminating large estates as a system contrary to justice, the general interest and social peace in the field, [as well as] ensuring biodiversity, food security and the effective enforcement of environmental and food rights for the present and future generations" (RBV 2001b, p.01). Small producers gained legal rights regarding their cultivated lands (Article 20). Idle lands could be redistributed by the new National Land Institute: "Article 36. In order to establish the bases of rural development, the National Land Institute [*Instituto Nacional de Tierras*] will adopt the measures it deems pertinent for the transformation of all the lands located within the rural estates into productive economic units; in compliance with this mandate, it may rescue any land that is idle or uncultivated from his property." Expropriations would involve "peaceful negotiations" [*negociación amistosa*] (Article 75); as Enríquez observed, "in the case of an expropriation, the state is required to provide compensation for the affected property," this involving "a cash payment, government bonds, or a combination of the two" (Enríquez 2013, p.621). A new tax was imposed on underutilized lands (Article 101), and a new state enterprise was created so as to "develop, coordinate and supervise the State's business activities for the development of the agrarian sector." For such purposes, "it may create companies and other private entities that are necessary for the effective fulfillment of its purpose" (Article 152). Several procedural mechanisms followed in order to legally organize in the new decisions (for a broader discussion of the land reform, see Enríquez 2013).

Despite these progressive state policies, the macroeconomic policies during Chávez's first years were not appropriate. Table 3.1 shows selected macroeconomic features of the Venezuelan economy over the period. The first years of Chávez administrations saw intense GDP fluctuations (see Fig. 3.1.); the government implemented moderate fiscal policies, which remained at constant levels until 2000 (deficits of 1,7% of the GDP between 1999 and 2000). However, low interest rates were

Table 3.1 Venezuela. Macroeconomic indicators. 1999–2018

Years	Exports of goods and services	Imports of goods and services	External debt (% of the GDP)	Overall fiscal balance of the central government (% of GDP)	Annual variation of consumer prices index: food (%)	Nominal lending rate (December)	Consumer prices (2010 = 100%)
1999	22.3	18.6	41	−1.7	20	28.1	11.5
2000	34.7	21.3	33	−1.7	13	22	13.3
2001	28.1	23.8	31	−4.4	12	27.7	15.0
2002	27.7	17.2	42	−4	31	33.9	18.4
2003	28.1	13.9	51	−1.9	17	19.5	24.1
2004	40.7	21.5	37	1.6	19	17.1	29.3
2005	57.1	29.3	30	0	14	15.4	34.0
2006	67.1	39.5	23	3	17	15.9	38.6
2007	72.1	58.3	25	−1.2	22	22	45.8
2008	98.2	64.4	21	5	31	22.2	60.3
2009	60.6	54.9	31	−3.6	26	19.1	77.5
2010	68.7	56.1	35	−4	27	18.1	100
2011	95.5	69.4	35	−4	24	16	127.1
2012	100.1	85.3	37	−2	19	16	154.0
2013	90.9	76.4	39	−1.19	56	15.7	231.3
2014	76.5	63.9	50	−1.9	68	19.3	348.2
2015	38.8	47.1	100	NA	180	20.9	772
2016	28.6	25.8	74	NA	274	22.3	2740.3
2017	34.9	19.3	97	NA	862	21.8	14,745.9
2018	34.4	19.8	86	NA	130,060	21.5	9654733.4

Source: Cepal-Stat (National Economic Profile). For interest rates, see Cepal-Stat, "Nominal lending rate, annual percentage." For consumer prices, see "Annual consumer prices indices – general level"

implemented in line with overvalued exchange rates in the face of inflation: consumer prices reached 29% in 2004 and 34% in 2005, but exchange rates were devaluated only by 20% and 11% over the same period (for inflation, see Table 3.1. above; for exchange rates, see Table 3.2). The economic policies would show a higher tolerance for credit expansion by means of declining interest rates but under an over-appreciated exchange rate system which would not stimulate investments vis-à-vis imports. Consumption rates were expanded in relative terms, the rate of investments in terms of the GDP dropping accordingly (see Sect. 4.2, Fig. 4.2).

Venezuela suffered the impacts of the American crisis of 2001 (the so-called dot-com bubble) in the form of lower exports between 2001 and 2002.[4] As exports

[4] The US total imports from Venezuela dropped from US$ 19,192 million in 2000 to US$ 15,958 million in 2001 (i.e., 20% less). Total exports to the United States reached still lower levels by 2002 (15 million), exports partially recovering only by 2003 (when they reached 17.6 million). As we

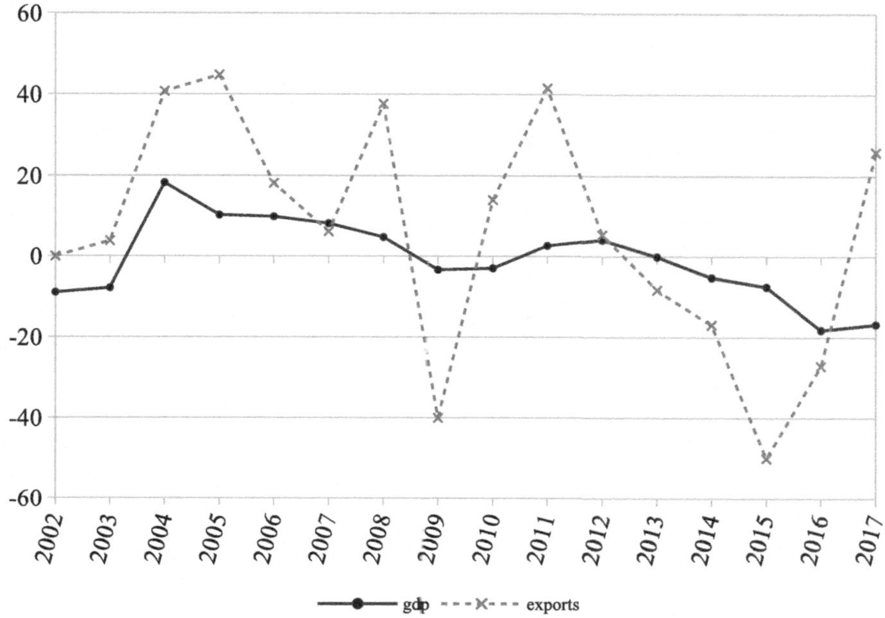

Fig. 3.1 Venezuela. GDP and exports (% annual change). 2002–2017. (Source: ECLAC 2019)

dropped with the impacts of the American crisis of 2001, the fiscal deficit was raised to −4,4% of the GDP, mainly because taxes dropped with falling exports and GDP recession (see Fig. 3.1). The higher trade surplus obtained in 2002 was achieved by a drop in imports caused by the ongoing economic recession, which lasted until 2003 and drove imports to only US$ 13 billion. The strikes in PDVSA since 2002 also affected oil exports, but as imports stagnated, a high trade surplus was reached. The external debt dropped between 1999 and 2001 but rose again in relative terms during the impacts on Venezuela of the American crisis; the external debt reached 42% of the GDP in 2002 and 51% in 2003.

It would be the recover in oil exports after 2003 that changed the external conditions of the economy and particularly for the state budget; this was possible not only because of the government's actions to face the strikers in PDVSA in 2002–2003 but also because of (1) the recovering of the American economy connected with (2) higher oil prices (they would hit US$ 90 per barrel by 2007). The GDP would follow these best conditions in oil markets between 2003 and 2008 (both in physical as in price terms), and this new scenario would lead to the improvement of fiscal conditions until 2009 (see Fig. 3.1). This new scenario in oil markets opened new

shall see, the higher amounts were reached in 2008 (52.2 million), these numbers coinciding with the higher amount of foreign reserves in Venezuela (see Fig. 2 of Preface). See Chap. 4 and also <www.bea.gov>, "International Transactions, International Services, and International Investment Position Tables"; Table 1.5, "US International Trade in goods and services by area and country – Venezuela"; and also Fig. 4.6.

Table 3.2 Venezuela. Main *Bolívares*/US$ dollar rates of exchange on 31 December. 2003–2018

	CADIVI								
	Buying rate	Selling rate							
2003	1596	1600							
2004	1915	1920							
2005	2144	2150							
2006	2144	2150							
2007	2.14	2.15							
2008	2.14	2.15							
2009	2.14	2.15							
								"Dólar preferencial" (then DIPRO)	
								Buying rate	
2010	4.28	4.3						2.6	
2011	4.28	4.3						N.A.	
2012	4.28	4.3						N.A.	
2013	6.28	4.3						N.A.	
			SICAD	**SICAD II**				N.A.	
			Buying rate/ selling rate	Buying rate	Selling rate			N.A.	
2014	6.28	6.3	12	49.8	49.9			N.A.	
						Convenios cambiarios (DICOM)		N.A.	
						Buying rate	Selling rate	N.A.	
2015	6.28	6.3	13.5	51.97	52.10	198.2	198.69	N.A.	

								DIPRO	
								Buying rate	Selling rate
2016	–	–	13.5	–	–	672.0	673.76	9.97	10.0
2017	–	–	13.5	–	–	3.336,63	3.345,0	9.97	10.0
	Managed float								
2018	636.5	638.1	–	–	–	–	–	–	–

Source: Estimated by the author according to data furnished by the Central Bank of Venezuela. *Observation: between 2007 and August 2018, *Bolívar Fuerte*; from August 2018 initially *Bolívar Soberano*; since 2019, simply *Bolívar*

[a]Acronyms: *CADIVI* Comisión Nacional de Administración de Divisas (National Commission for Exchange Rate Administration), *SICADI* Sistema Cambiario Alternativo de Divisas (Alternative System of Exchange Rates), *Convenio Cambiario* currency regulation, *Dólar preferencial* subsidized dollar, *DIPRO* Operaciones de Divisas con tipo de cambio protegido (subsized exchange rate transactions), *DICOM* Sistema de Divisas de Tipo de Cambio Complementario Flotante de Mercado (complementary floating exchange rate regime). A new parallel rate was introduced in 2015 through SIMADI (*Sistema Marginal de Divisas* [Marginal System of Exchange Rate]). *N.A.* not available on Central Bank's website

perspectives for the implementation of the type of progressive policies which Chávez's pursued: Venezuela would reach an accumulated amount of US$ 243 billion dollars between 2002 and 2009 in total exports. But these progressive policies would not be coupled with real macroeconomic incentives for domestic production, the economy keeping its dependence on the (dropping) rate of growth in oil exports. And they would face a huge political opposition, which led to the coup attempt in 2002.

3.3 Coup Attempt and the Socialist Turn (2002–2008)

As it could be expected when regarding a Latin American nation, those new progressive legislations and policies implemented by Chávez's first presidential terms faced the fierce opposition of the traditional political forces, which lost influence in the aftermath of the rise of the MVR. These opposition tendencies were converted into a political coup attempt in April 2002. Chávez was kidnapped, and Pedro Carmona, former president of *Fedecámaras* (the conservative Venezuelan Federation of Chambers of Commerce and Production), assumed power for 1 day – for the ephemeral rejoice of the bourgeoisie.[5] A massive popular support by the *Chavistas* on the streets and in the army prevented the success of the *coup*. Chávez returned and Pedro Carmona, after the embarrassing defeat, left to Colombia. The government also faced a major strike in PDVSA between 2002 and 2003, which had great economic consequences in terms of falling oil revenues and fiscal crisis. Once in power again, Chávez reacted by punishing those involved in the failed coup (including the members of the army) as well as the strikers. This increased the ranks of opposition, while PDVSA (and the economy) had to cope with the negative consequences of the purge, in terms of a temporary lack of managerial capacity and falling production.

The government also began to expropriate private enterprises which, allegedly, were not functioning well – particularly those suspected of speculation and planned underinvestments. These measures frightened the domestic private groups, particularly those which had not political links with the government (for a discussion, see Yaffe 2015 and Curcio 2016). Be that as it may, in the eve of the rising of the commodity prices over the 2000s, PDVSA's revenues were put under official control, and they now should contribute directly to the social and economic development. This was a right decision, from the point of view of controlling the main economic surplus of the nation (for a theoretical defense, see the classic discussion of Baran 1957 and also Robinson 1979). By means of the new FONDESPA (*Fondo para el Desarrollo Económico y Social del País*' [National Development Fund]), a share of PDVSA's profits would now support directly the economic and social decisions of

[5] Some argue he was poisoned during the event; for an account of the 2003 coup, see Kovalik 2019 and Bartley and O'Brian 2003 and Golinger 2006.

the government (see PDVSA 2011 and 2016). This gave the new administration a much deeper control of the main source of economic surplus in the nation, something which would allow for a higher discretionary capacity of the economic policy. The government also raised taxes on foreign oil companies, from 1% to 16%. These measures were a true heresy for the neoliberal rules of the game. Accordingly, they were depicted by neoliberal authors as a regression in terms of PDVSA's business profile (see Corrales and Penfold 2011 and Gallegos 2016). From the point of view of Chávez's supporters, PDVSA was now being transformed into a public enterprise, which should finance development and social goals.

After these events, Chávez made a decisive turn; he began to "raise the flag of socialism" in order to mobilize political support under a more radical perspective. Accordingly, the new economic guidelines after 2003 were condensed in the *First Socialist Plan of the Nation – Simón Bolívar National Project* (RBV 2007). This plan was published in 2007 and had a clearer "socialist" feature. It reflected Chávez's ideas on socialism, which did not include central planning and quantitative targets for each enterprise; at the same time, it was reasonably advanced in terms of a heterodox approach for the Venezuelan economic development. The document proposed the adoption of a so-called new socialist ethics (p.5) and, through social equality, the achievement of the "ultimate social happiness" (p.9), in line with Bolívar and Simón Rodriguez's writings.[6] The plan also argued that health services should be free for all.[7] "Revolutionary protagonistic democracy" should be made by communal councils (*consejos comunales*) participating in economic decisions (p.13); the social control of mass media should be reinforced.[8] Venezuela should use its oil reserves to diversify the economy,[9] constructing a new "socialist productive model," also proposing a new global order toward multipolarity.[10] This "new economic model" should be based mainly on the so-called social production firms (*empresas de producción social*; for a discussion, see Azzellini 2009):

> Social Production Enterprises [SPE] are economic entities dedicated to the production of goods or services in which work has its own meaning, not alienated and authentic, [in which] there is no social discrimination at work and of any type of work, [as well as] no

[6] "The supreme social happiness is the long-term vision which has as its starting point the construction of an inclusive social structure, creating a new society of included, a new social, productive, socialist, humanistic, endogenous model, where we all live in similar conditions towards what Simón Bolívar said: 'The Supreme Social Happiness'" (RBV 2007, p.9).

[7] Among the goals involving the "supreme social happiness" was to "expand and consolidate the health services in a suitable [*oportuna*] and free manner [*forma*]" (RBV 2007, p.11).

[8] Regarding communication services, "protagonistic democracy" should "strengthen the media and information of the State and democratize its communication spaces" (RBV 2007, p.20).

[9] "Accelerate oil seeding, deepening the internalization of hydrocarbons to strengthen productive diversification and social inclusion" (RBV 2007, p.41).

[10] Chávez observed on page 4 (presentation): "The construction of a multipolar world implies the creation of new poles of power that represent the breakdown of unipolar hegemony, in the search for social justice, solidarity and guarantees of peace, while deepening fraternal dialogue among peoples, their self-determination and respect for freedom of thought" (RBV 2007, p.4).

> privileges at work associated with the hierarchical position, [achieving] substantive equality among its members, based on participatory and protagonistic planning. (RBV 2007, p.21)

However, state and capitalist enterprises should not be abolished, although they should assume social responsibilities ("social responsibility of private enterprise," p.8):

> The Socialist Productive Model will be basically made up of Social Production Enterprises, which constitute the germ and the path towards Socialism of the 21st Century, although State companies and private capitalist companies will persist. In the SPE the workers will appropriate the resulting economic surplus, which will be distributed in proportion to the amount of work contributed; the management will be democratic and participatory and the relative weight of the participation will be based on the person and not on the basis of the capital contributed. The SPE will emerge from the multiplication and growth of successful experiences of existing associative units, which will be established as a result of State action, and the transformation of State enterprises or private capitalist enterprises into SPE. (RBV 2007, p.21–22)

At the same time, the document reinstated the necessity for the state to control the oil production and its correlated by-products. Large states should be abolished and food sovereignty should be achieved. A new territorial organization should overcome the concentration of production and population off the cost, through new "axes of economic development" linking the western and northeastern part of the territory (*eje Llanero*), focusing also on smaller- and medium-size cities. The Venezuelan share of Amazonia should be preserved as an environmental and hydrological reserve. With regard to energy production, the document (wrongly) foresaw a growing demand of the Venezuelan oil. This prevision wrongly supposed stable or even growing oil exports to the United States (see Chap. 4).

After the coup attempt in 2003, the government intensified its social policies; a new literacy plan was created (*Missión Robinson*), as well as a new approach to extending medical services on a local (communal) level (*Missión Barrio adentro*); small and medium enterprises were stimulated and supported by new discretionary means under the *Vuelvan Caras* project. By 2005, the United Nations declared that Venezuela was free from illiteracy. Presidential Decree 3.645 created a special commission for the prevention of all forms of racial discrimination. In this context, the opposition then started to organize a referendum which would lead to Chávez dismissal (an institutional mechanism allowed by the new constitution). After many legal interruptions, the referendum was made on 15 August 2004, Chávez winning with 5.8 million votes (the opposition reached 3.9 million).

On 4 December 2006, new elections took place, including the national assembly. *Acción Democrática* and the other opposition parties boycotted them; Chávez, running against Manuel Rosales (representing the broad conservative coalition *Un novo tiempo*), won again. The national assembly was now dominated by his supporters. In light of that, the government advanced in terms of its political project. The legislation regarding the *consejos comunales* –communal councils – was introduced. The government implemented more nationalizations, such as the *Compañia Autónoma de Teléfonos de Venezuela* (CANTV), *Electricidad de Caracas*, *Lácteos los Andes*, *Banco de Venezuela*, and cement firms, now obliged to sell 50% of the total production to the domestic markets. The government would also create a national wide food supply network (PDVAL) in order to cope with inflation and scarcity. These actions led to an enormous flow of critiques and reactions.[11]

The year of 2007 saw the opening of new concluded projects: Venezuela paid off its debt with the World Bank; the Orinoco Petroleum Belt was nationalized; a new transport system was inaugurated in Mérida; tests for academic requirements to the admission in the national universities were abolished; a new university for experimental arts (UNEARTE) was created. The government also tried to introduce a constitutional reform, including unlimited reelections of the president (the constitutional allowed one reelection), new socialist types of property, and a new constitutional socialist orientation for the nation as whole. This constitutional reform was not approved by the voters (abstention reached 45%).

Despite this political turn, the macroeconomic tools did not foster domestic production. Inflation rates permanently grew over the period, consumer prices going from 11% by 1999 to 18% in 2002 and from 24% in 2003 to 29% in 2004. The nominal rates of interest dropped between all the interlude 1999 and 2007, showing the CBV's tolerant stance toward lending rates in the overall economy. Accordingly, real interest rates showed a permanent drop since then. At the same time, we saw that the *Bolívar* under CADIVI was not properly devaluated between 2004 and 2005; this path was not changed. Inflation reached 38% in 2006, 45% in 2007, and 60% in 2008, but exchange rates were fixed at 2150 *Bolívares* between 2005 and 2006 and fixed again between 2007 and 2009 under a new monetary standard: facing the rising inflation, the government implemented a monetary reform in 2007, by means of the new *Bolívar Fuerte* (parity of 1000/1 with regard to the old *Bolívar*), as well as price controls. This new nominal appreciation of the *Bolívar* contributed to an increase in imports between 2007 and 2008, as consumer prices reached 45% in 2007 and 60% in 2008.

3.4 From the Impacts of the 2008 Crisis to Chávez's Death (2008–2013)

The administration maintained a moderate fiscal policy before the 2008–2009 international crisis and the subsequent drop in oil prices, with consolidated fiscal surpluses. Exchange rates would be fixed until the creation of SICAD I and II in 2014 (which devaluated the *Bolívar* within very limited terms in face of the accumulated

[11] See Wilpert (2007) for a defense of Chávez's economic policies; for useful critiques, though under commonsense and deceptive neoliberal critiques, see Corrales and Penfold (2011) and Gallegos (2016); for moderate critiques, see Di John 2009; for an initial defense of the alleged socialist orientation of the economy, see Dieterich 2005 [one of Chávez most radical supporters who broke with *Bolivarianism* afterward]; for a recent theoretical defense of the Venezuelan policies, see Vasapollo 2013; for a detailed and honest account of the initial aspects of the current Venezuelan crisis, see Weisbrot 2015.

past inflation). The over-appreciated exchange rate system was deepened by the creation of "preferential dollar" regime (DIPRO) by 2009. Accordingly, imports, which reached more than 50% of the GDP in 2003, hit the same level again in 2008 (see Fig. 4.3). Despite the alleged orientation toward autonomy and diversification of the economy, the decisive macroeconomic tools boosted consumption and imports, which were raised in terms of the GDP, in parallel, as we shall see, with manufacturing and agriculture lagging behind (see Chap. 4). That is, in that context, the macroeconomic disarray referred to a high inflation coupled with an overvalued exchange rate, and not fiscal deficits. According to the compilation made by Cepal-Stat (see Table 3.1), overall fiscal surpluses were attained between 2005 and 2009. External and domestic public debts dropped from 18% and 29% of the GDP by 2003 to 7.5% and 10% in 2008 (respectively). The national external debt also dropped from 51% to 21% between 2003 and 2008. But the exchange rate would remain fixed between 2010 and 2013 under CADIVI; the "preferential dollar" rate (DIPRO) was still more overvalued. This over-appreciated rate of exchange occurred despite the underlying inflationary tendencies, which should have led to a devaluation of the national currency in order to prevent an appreciation *vis-à-vis* the dollar. In practical terms, the over-appreciation of the *Bolívar* was used as a tool against inflation, particularly in the form of cheap goods from abroad and as a form of granting indirect privileges to the foreign enterprises, which sent abroad their domestic profits without large losses in terms of the national currency. This policy for exchange rates also suggests that the government apparently finally admitted a fixed although declining demand curve for the oil exports; this implied that the devaluation of the national currency would be useless in order to boost more exports, only leading to losses in the terms of trade (for a critical discussion of the role of exchange rates in this context, see Dachevsky and Kornblihtt 2016; for the oil sector, see the next chapter).

Table 3.2 shows the recent evolution of the exchange rate regimes in Venezuela, as informed by the Central Bank of Venezuela on its several sources available on its web page. As it can be seen, despite nominal devaluations between 2003 and 2006, the *Bolívar* remained over-appreciated under CADIVI until 2010, when the government inaugurated a dual system; the CADIVI system devaluated with moderation the *Bolívar*, but the old parity was maintained by the system of *dólar preferencial* ("preferential dollar," subsequently "DIPRO"). The new exchange rate under CADIVI was kept until 2013; there is no data regarding DIPRO after 2011, but all evidence suggest that it was also kept overvalued.[12] By 2016, 1 dollar still costed

[12] "[A]fter a serious devaluation of the bolivar in the context of the 1989 crisis there was a revaluation. With Chávez's first term this revaluation intensified, reaching a peak of 459 per- cent overvaluation in 2010. Since then, despite the successive nominal devaluations of the local currency, it has remained overvalued in relation to parity and has become the principal mechanism of appropriation of petroleum ground rent. From 2010 to the end of 2015, the bolivar underwent a nominal devaluation of 43 percent, but monetary liquidity rose by 1100 percent and inflation by 600 percent. The result of these imbalances was greater overvaluation, reaching 1586 percent in 2015" (Dachevsky and Kornblihtt 2016, p.9). This work makes an interesting discussion of the consequences of the overvaluation of the Venezuelan domestic currency over the period 1998–2016.

9,97 *Bolívares* under the DIPRO system, despite the high past inflation rates. Since 2009, the mixed results of a drop in reserves and revenues coming from lower exports, followed by a fiscal deficit, as well as growing speculation with stocks of tangible goods (an underlying struggle against the government), all drove inflation to still higher levels (for a discussion, see Salas Rodríguez 2014 and Curcio 2016).

It can be seen that the impacts of the 2008–2009 crisis were severe, constituting the first stage of the Venezuelan multiple external crises since then. According to Cepal-Stat, the current account balance as a percentage of GDP reached only 0.1% in 2009 (having reached 14% in 2006 and 5% in 2007), and net foreign investments (which were already low) were negative for this year. Exports in 2009 reached only 60% regarding 2008 but imports 84%. Facing these impacts, the administration reduced the value-added tax (IVA) from 14% to 11% and issued new debt in 2009, selling new *Bonos Soberanos* (total of US$ 3 billion; for a summary of the main economic and political decisions over the period, see RBV 2019).

Exchange controls were maintained, and nominal rates of interest were increased until 2010.[13] The government fought speculation and implemented other plans, such as *Fundo Bicentenário para pequenas empresas* and *Plan Viviendas*. As already mentioned, by 2010, a subsidized exchange rate for imports (DIPRO) was introduced (US$ 1/*Bs* 2.6; see Table 3.2), as well as a national plan against speculation and the creation of alternative markets for distribution. Foreign trade improved somewhat in 2011, but external conditions were not good; PDVSA and the government as well issued new debt in foreign and domestic markets (US$ 3 billion and *Bs.* $ 45 billion, respectively, RBV 2019). According to Cepal-Stat, the central government saw a third consecutive fiscal deficit in 2011, now reaching 4% of the GDP. Venezuela's revenue services (SENIAT) were reformed and improved so as to combat taxa evasion (see RBV 2019).

Chávez run for a new reelection in 2012 while suffering from cancer. The rates of economic growth were dropping, and there were not so good economic perspectives. The GDP showed negative results for 2008–2009, and only a small recovery between 2011 and 2012; then, it started to go down without stop (until 2018). The crisis in the balance of payments deepened, and trade (and fiscal) deficits started to grow over time. The Central Bank repatriated 150 tons in gold reserves as an auxiliary measure to counter the speculation against the new *Bolívar Fuerte* (see RBV 2019). According to Cepal-Stat, public debt was rising, the fiscal deficit reaching 4.9% in terms of the GDP; only 20% of the population regarded the evolution of the economy in positive terms at that moment.[14] The official rate of unemployment reached 8%. In parallel, oil and gas fields were discovered (in Orinoco) and new (state) enterprises were founded. According to official data, social security was extended and reached 1.7 million people (RBV 2019). Exchange rates would be

[13] They were lowered again until 2014. See Cepal-Stat, "Tase de interés activa nominal."

[14] A positive evaluation of the economy reached 57% of the population in 2007; see Cepal-Stat, Venezuela, "The Way the Market Functions: Positive Evaluation of the Country's Economy by Sex."

kept overvalued until Chávez's death in 2013, when SICAD I and II introduced a higher devaluation of the *Bolívar*, though a very limited one.

In this context, new legislations for land and labor were introduced. Regarding the former, the law passed in 2001 was reformed toward a more progressive feature (see RBV 2010). It was still more advanced in social terms, as it declared that private lands should be submitted to the national food security (Article 2). Agrarian activities should be based on self-management and communal councils (*autogestión* and *consejos comunales*). Underutilized large states were considered as opposing public interests; their existence should be communicated to the authorities, expropriations being imposed when necessary (Articles 7, 35, and 70). Public lands belonging to the National Institute for Land should benefit and be distributed to peasants who "have the will and disposition to agricultural work in harmony with the dispositions of the Executive power" (Article 13). Peasants who occupied a piece of land for more than 3 years gained the right to stay permanently and receive official support (Article 17). The INTI would also be on charge of evaluating the agrarian conditions of the nation in order to foster domestic production. A new public enterprise would be created to "consolidate the participation of the Venezuela in the production, distribution and trade (domestic and external) of food" (Article 146).

As an additional attempt to counter discontent before a new presidential election, a new labor legislation was also enacted by the national assembly. It was called *Ley Orgánica del Trabajo de los Trabajadores y Trabajadoras* (LOTTT; see RBV 2012, p.01). Its self-declared aim was to recover Venezuela from the neoliberal dismantling of labor rights. From a socialist point of view, LOTTT was not a radical labor legislation. It aimed to protect workers under a now mixed economy, while wage-earning relations would not be abolished, as well as labor mobility. It was a progressive step. Equality between men and women in terms of all labor rights was established; subcontracting and unfair dismissal were prohibited; public social security was guaranteed as a universal right. At the same time, foreign employees should be limited to 5% of the existing labor force in any firm, and their wages should not exceed 20% of the other wages. As labor mobility would be normally accepted, employment contracts could range from permanent to temporary (Article 60). The implementation of LOTTT was certainly one of the reasons why Chávez and Maduro still retained significant popular support.

Despite of all political and economic changes since 2003, Chávez was not satisfied. Maybe this could be explained by personal reasons (his sickness), but surely also because of the economic conditions of the nation. Despite nationalizations, growing subsidies, and capital transfers from state budget since 2004, the decline in the share of manufacturing deepened since 2007, imports as a share of the GDP reaching 51% by the end of 2012 (instead of 21% in 2003[15]); the economy still fluctuated under the swings of oil exports. The Venezuelan bourgeoisie had lost the political control of the state, but these 15 years had not been enough to alter in

[15] See BCV, Table 5.2.7, "Oferta y demanda global a precios de 1997 - Bolívares, Producto interno bruto petrolero y no petrolero."

qualitative terms the structure of the economy. Thus, Chávez recognized, 1 year before his death, that Venezuela was far from "socialism." He observed on 20 October 2012 at Miraflores Palace in Caracas:

> I have signed a decree creating a kind of superior organization [*ente*] for the communes. Where is it? It have not worked. [Well, it is from] the commune, the people's power [*that we will find solutions*], not from Miraflores nor from this or that Ministry. We shall not believe that we are ready because we will inaugurate the Cerro Azul Cement Factory or the factory of factories [sic] in Guanare, or a computer factory, a satellite factory etc., or because we simply nationalize the cement industry…. (Chávez Frías 2012, p.18–21)

This was a truism, but Chávez was obviously trying to influence the future course of the events. The government seemed to assure a firm control of the army and National Bolivarian Guard, as well as the National Assembly (until 2016), but the president called for self-criticism and a reinforcement of local and democratic structures of power through the *comunas* (see Chávez Frías 2012).

In that context, Chávez won one more presidential election with 55% of the valid votes in October 2012 over Henrique Capriles, representing the broad and conservative coalition *Mesa de Unidad Democrática* (MUD) – which shared the same features of other Latin American conservative and rightist forces (elitism, pro-imperialists, etc.). A new government plan was formulated, the *Plan Patria 2013–2019* (RBV 2013). This wordy document essentially reinstated the same perspectives of the last 2007 plan, displaying a socialist message mixed with a neo-structuralist approach which emphasized the need for import substitution and diversification of the economy, in a now mixed Venezuelan economy where state's share in the overall economy was growing. The unrealistic macroeconomic goals of annual growth rates of 3–4% and inflation rates of 20% would not be achieved over the following years; at the same time, the plan clearly contradicted the existing system of exchange rates, which incredibly was not mentioned.

Chávez's health conditions did not improve. He died on 5 March 2013 amidst great anxiety among his supporters, before being able to assume power. Nicolás Maduro, then vice president, took power temporarily as an interim, being elected president through new elections in April 2018. In this context, there was a broad opposition spectrum that hoped to profit from Chávez's death. It included the opposing political parties, the "anti-Chavista" political left, a large share of the local bourgeoisie and middle classes, the "anti-Chavista" share of the working classes, Colombian paramilitaries and drug dealers, and the government of the United States. As with Tito in Yugoslavia or Perón in Argentina, the death of the charismatic leader, coupled with an underlying economic crisis, would be followed by social unrest and political conflict.

3.5 Maduro's First Presidency (2013–2018)

Nicolás Maduro is usually described with all sorts of class prejudices because of his working class origins (he worked as a bus driver and also as a left-wing trade unionist). However, Maduro was not inexperienced in state and economic affairs. He in fact stood on Chávez's side since the beginning of the MVR movement and was one of his closest allies. Maduro presided over PDVSA, acted as a national deputy and then as the president of the National Assembly. He was also Chávez's Minister of Foreign Affairs between 2006 and 2012 and then Chávez's vice president in 2013. Unlike many vice presidents in Latin America (Julio Cobos, Michel Temer, Lenin Moreno, etc.), he showed total commitment to the "Bolivarian Project." However, he was not charismatic as Chávez and would govern under much more harsh conditions, which would reinforce his difficulties.

He took office temporarily in March 2013 while Chávez was under medical treatment. After Chávez's death, Maduro won another election (on 14 April 2013), reaching 50,78% of the total valid votes; Henrique Capriles, from *Primero Justicia/ Mesa de Unidad Democrática*, got 49%. By the end of 2013, Chávez former *Plan de la Pátria* ("Second socialist plan of economic and social development 2013–2019") was announced and endorsed (RBV 2013). It stressed "Bolivarian socialism," national independence, the need for a new international order, participative democracy, and the need for a sustainable growth (in ecological terms).[16] The announced macroeconomic goals involved an annual average rate of 3–4% for the GDP growth, maximum annual inflation rates of 20%, the extraction of 3 million oil barrels in 2013 and 9 million by 2019, as well as the increase in social indicators (wealth distribution, education levels, child mortality) and the alleged maintenance of an industrial and agricultural policies (this last stressing food sovereignty and a "socialist" model for agriculture, though imports of cheap foodstuff and other primary goods by means of the subsidized rate of exchange [DIPRO] conflicted with them). These macroeconomic goals were highly unrealistic, extraction of oil reaching only 1,5 million per day by 2018, in parallel with economic recession, worsening conditions of living, and ongoing dependence on food imports.

The opposition tried to benefit from the apparent fragility of the new administration, and violence spread, with several deaths. *Guarimbas* (violent street barricades organized by young criminals, supported by the opposition) spread. This led to strong responses from the police and the army and decaying rates of popularity in the midst of a violent social climate. The opposition, colluded with Colombian and American interests, tried to undermine what seemed to be a fragile new administration by means of violence, speculation, traffic of goods, and other criminal methods. In this context, former Minister Luis Salas described with details the difficulties faced by the government when trying to implement price controls as a way to

[16] The Ministry for "Eco-socialism" would be created afterward (2014), though the offshore drilling of oil represented a growing threat to the environment, as well as the pattern of exports which should finance domestic growth (nonrenewable crude oil).

combat speculation and economic terrorism[17]; according to him, disobediences of price controls had begun already in 2010 (Salas Rodríguez 2014, p. 76[18]). In light of this, the government launched the *Órgano Superior para Defensa Popular de la Economía* (OSDPE), a decision which intended to guarantee the food supply as well as stable prices through more state controls and supervisions against speculation. Moreover, minimum wages were raised by 30% in 2013 (see RBV 2019), while inflation grew by 56% (according to Cepal-Stat). Nominal interest rates continued to drop since 2009, reaching 15%; fiscal deficits reached 2% of the GDP, while total credit grew from 40 to 49% of the GDP (ECLAC 2018). Despite these expansive efforts, there would be no GDP growth in 2013, as exports dropped 8%, and the private sector intensified speculation and smuggling (including importing under DIPRO and reselling these goods in Colombia for higher prices). But the PSUV won the municipal elections in December.

The political and economic situation became worse in 2014. The government established a maximum of 30% for private profits as an auxiliary tool against speculation (RBV 2019). There was a new wave of violence, with 43 deaths and attacks in infrastructure and facilities, particularly universities. In this context, national deputy Robert Serra (PSUV) and his partner were brutally murdered, allegedly with the support of Colombian paramilitaries (this hypothesis seems to be endorsed by Ciccariello-Maher 2016, p.108). Total exports, whose rates of growth in fact were falling since 2005, dropped regarding the previous year (from US$ 90 to US$ 76 billion). The *Bolívar* suffered successive devaluations, in official terms but specially in parallel markets. Inflation and exchange rate controls were reinforced in the face of falling reserves combined with speculation. Inflation was also reinforced by a growing monetization of the official expenditures (see ECLAC 2019, p.88). Given the ongoing drop in the GDP and the domestic savings, which led to higher foreign loans, the external debt grew from 39% to 50% of the GDP. By means of the new SICAD I and II, the government implemented a nominal devaluation of the Bolívar vis-à-vis the dollar; CADIVI remained fixed until 2015. There would be a much more realistic devaluation by DICOM in 2015. (The nation then had five different exchange rate regimes.)

To make things worse, oil prices began to drop in June 2014, from US$ 106 by January to US$ 53 by December. The price of the Venezuelan oil barrel would reach only US$ 20 by mid-2015. Moniz Bandeira suggests that this drop was a result of Saudi-American veiled intentions to damage Russia, Iran, and also Venezuela (Moniz Bandeira 2016, p.611). This trend was mixed with changes in the American domestic energy markets, originated by *fracking* methods and other new technologies, which led to falling imports of the Venezuelan oil (particularly crude oil). International reserves, which reached US$ 42 billion in 2009, amounted to only US$ 21 billion by mid-2014. One could ask: How those 240 US$ billion in oil

[17] For terrorism and sabotage, see also Maduro's successive annual reports before the National Assembly, Supreme Court, and then Constituent Assembly (*Memória y Cuenta*, 2013–2018).

[18] However, data related to disobedience of price controls, mentioned by this author, could not be found on INE's website.

exports were used since 2003 if domestic production and consumption were reaching so dramatic levels? Since 2003, Venezuela had achieved again one of the higher rates of foreign reserves in the region, but – such as once described by Furtado – the high propensity to import of the economy and the government's incapacity of maintaining at least a part of these resources through more determined methods had led to a new crisis in the balance of payments when oil markets crashed.

The drop in oil prices coupled with lower physical exports had automatic impacts in terms of fiscal imbalances and falling demand and lower production rates in PDVSA and revenues. Central government's debt, which amounted to 4.5% of the GDP in 2008, reached 19.5% in 2014, along with one more overall fiscal deficit (1.9% of the GDP in 2014). Facing the contraction, the administration decided to deep expansionary measures. Nominal rates of interest remained on the same levels (17%), and as consumer prices grew by 68%, there were real negative interest rates, domestic credit reaching 59% of the GDP (see ECLAC 2018). Required reserves held by the Central Bank were lowered in absolute terms, this trend lasting until mid-2016.[19] In parallel, new special economic zones with the granting of especial fiscal incentives were launched in Paranaguá and Ureña, San Antonio, while foreign investments remained almost null since 2013 (RBV 2019). According to the CepalStat, extreme poverty grew by 7.5% between 2008 and 2014, poverty now officially reaching 28% of the population.

In the beginning of 2015, Maduro travelled to gather with OPEC leaders, so as to negotiate and try to find solutions for the crisis in the oil markets. The perspectives were not good. According to the OPEC, "sharp decline in oil prices witnessed at the end of last year [2014] and the start of this year [were] caused by oversupply and speculation" (OPEC, 167th meeting, June 2015). The conference also observed that "the recent build in stocks and the surplus of oil in both OECD and non-OECD countries, which has resulted in stock levels that lie well above the five-year average in terms of absolute volumes, indicates that the market is comfortably supplied" (OPEC, 167th meeting, June 2015). In this context, by mid-2015, former American President Barack Obama issued a decree declaring Venezuela a "national security threat," sanctions on several Venezuelan officials following his announcement. Skirmishes between the Venezuelan army and Colombian paramilitaries led to the closure of the frontiers in San Antonio de Táchira, Zure and Apuche, as the administration in Caracas denounced the smuggling of money, food, and other goods into the Colombian territory. Minimum wages were raised by 60%, but gasoline prices were adjusted so as to help PDVSA's budget.

Almost as a direct result of the declining conditions of life, a decisive political watershed happened by the end of 2015: an electoral defeat for PSUV in the legislative elections for the National Assembly of deputies. The opposition – the coalition *Mesa de Unidad Democrática* (MUD) – won the elections for the national assembly in December, winning 109 seats in a total of 167. This fact caused a turning point in

[19] See BCV, Table 1.3.23, "Encaje legal y reservas bancarias, bancos comerciales, milliones de Bolívares."

the political climate. The government officially recognized the results, but feared that the doors were opened to a political maneuver against the presidency. This suspicion seemed to be confirmed when Ramos Allup (national deputy of *Acción Democrática* [AD]) ordered the removal of Chávez's portrait inside the National Assembly. The PSUV then reacted, denouncing as fraudulent the election of several deputies. The National Assembly ignored these denounces and maintained its functions, which pointed toward growing criticism of Maduro. There was then a quick reaction on behalf of the Supreme Court (*Tribunal Supremo de Justicia* [TSJ]): the National Assembly was closed (*desacato*). This fact originated a bizarre situation and successive conflicts, as state decisions would now be decided by the Supreme Court instead of the National Assembly, which, in turn, continued to deliberate and to struggle against the executive. In this context, the National Assembly tried to declare the nullity of a new decree of economic emergence signed by former Minister of Economy Luis Salas (PSUV).

At the same time, a new round of price and rate controls was established, along with mechanisms for rationing of food and other basic products through the *Comités Locales de Abastecimiento y Producción* (CLAPs). On 14 February 2016, a new "State of Economic Emergence" was published by the *Gazeta Oficial* (Decree 2.184), one of many over the following years. The government defined the economic environment as the result of an "economic war against socialism" (*guerra económica*) and acted accordingly. The decree, which would be renewed for several times, gave the government more instruments of intervention, such as the cancelation of the budget law of 2015, allowing for higher fiscal expenditures; the immediate recruitment of service servants, if needed; the immediate import of goods, now exempted from bureaucratic impediments; the immediate access to foreign reserves so as to import essential goods; the official right to dispose of all private infrastructure in order to distribute and deliver essential goods. The exchange rate system was altered again, becoming still more complicated: a floating rate was allowed to operate (DICOM), while DIPRO was maintained as the subsidized rate for imports of essential goods,[20] in parallel with a remaining complementary rate (SICAD and CADIVI). Official minimum wages were raised by 120% but consumer price indices reached 274% by the end of 2016, while nominal interest rates grew by 2%. The 500 and 20,000 *Bolívares* bills were created.

By May 2016, the opposition presented a request for a referendum against Maduro, formally allowed by the constitution. In September, the Supreme Court declared to be null all acts of the National Assembly; and in October, the National Electoral Council did not approve a referendum against Maduro. Riots and vandalism continued. The GDP contracted by 18% in 2016, amid ongoing disputes between the government and enterprises, which halted economic activity. Shrinking markets and the impossibility of accessing inputs and reserves were the alleged reasons for these closures, according to the enterprises; but the government declared

[20] As mentioned above, this rate of exchange would be abolished in 2018 in order to face speculation in parallel markets. See BCV, "Convenio Cambiario n.35," March 2016.

that these actions were illegal, a part of an economic sabotage. Some new nationalizations followed, such as the expropriation of the American Kimberly-Clark (hygiene products). Meanwhile, domestic lending to private sector more than doubled since 2013, reaching one of the highest rates in the region, while risk premiums on national bonds climbed, also reaching the highest levels in Latin America (ECLAC 2016, p.73 and p.205).

Violence and confusion were maintained in 2017. Following a ministerial reform and a new decree of economic emergence, the "old" National Assembly launched one more of its attacks, declaring that Maduro had abandoned his post as president. Ignoring the Assembly, Maduro spoke directly to the Supreme Court, presenting new economic measures in his *Memória y Cuenta de 2016* as the reopening of exchange offices and less income taxes for those receiving less than 6000 fiscal unities per month. The government also threatened to expropriate bakeries which were refusing to produce bread. The floating exchange rate of the *Bolívar* was devaluated by 60%, the national currency suffering extreme devaluations in parallel markets. In this context, the opposition organized mass demonstrations and collected signatures so as to legitimize the power of the now closed National Assembly.

In this chaotic environment, Maduro had many options at hand. He could resign, putting under risk the achievements of the Bolivarian policies and the return of the *esquálidos* (pejorative term for members of the right-wing opposition). He could impose an open dictatorship instead, but this option contradicted the legitimacy of the regime, still based on a (narrow) electoral majority. This option could not be simply ruled out, giving the fact that hostile forces were driving the nation to a virtual civil war. Maduro, however, opted for a middle-term decision, in line with the political traditional of *Chavismo*: he called for the election of a new National Constituent Assembly. This decision was ratified by the Supreme Court, which was on the side of the government. New elections occurred in July, with the participation of approximately 8 million people or 40% of the total registered voters. These results showed the ongoing support of a share of the population, but also a high apathy and the permanent political division, the opposition once again boycotting the process.

Following the elections, the powers of the old National Assembly – which refused to be closed – were officially transferred to the new National Constituent Assembly. Venezuela now had a dual legislative power, at least in nominal terms. By mid-2017, Maduro delivered new economic decisions. These measures included new concessions to foreign investments, higher taxes for the rich families, new price controls (*precios acordados*), the reopening of exchange agencies along the border with Colombia, a new rise of the minimum wage (40%), and a new state enterprise, *Consorcio Agroalimentario del Sur* (Agrosur), which should be on charge of developing the Venezuelan agriculture (see RBV 2019). These measures did not pacify the opposition. The prospects became even worse when on 25 August 2017 new American President D. Trump signed Executive Order 13808 with more sanctions against Venezuela, this time with much more serious consequences – as they prohibited the issuing of medium- and long-term debt to PDVSA and the Venezuelan government by any American entity.[21] The White House, in fact, had declared an open opposition to the Maduro administration (see White House 2019).

In October 2017, the PSUV officially won the regional elections, with 19 elected governors against four of the opposition; in December, new municipal elections occurred, with a new victory for the PSUV. But as usually, part of the opposition boycotted the dispute, and the legitimacy of these elections was not fully accepted. One of the last important economic decisions taken by Maduro in his first term was the creation of the *Petro*, an electronic currency issued by the Central Bank which would be backed by the Venezuelan oil reserves. Its price would be the equivalent of one oil barrel. This measure intended to counter the economic blockade arising from the new American sanctions, which would be confronted by exchanging import goods for oil. There were also new changes in the exchange rate regime, toward a unification of the existing exchange rates and the extinction of DIPRO, so as to lower the speculation in the parallel markets.[22]

As violence persisted, there were new intents of achieving agreements before the presidential election of 2018. The opposition knew that there was not much time before an eventual new electoral victory of Maduro, as the government now controlled all main state apparatus. Maduro in fact would be once again reelected, through anticipated elections in May 2018. Regarding the economic data, there are few available statistics for the 2017–2018 period, but it is clear that the general scenario was severe (null current account balance, null foreign investments, low terms of trade, and consumer prices exceeding 100,000%).[23] The hopes of a "socialism for the twenty-first century" seemed to be ending in total disappointment.

---

[21] See <https://www.state.gov/venezuela-related-sanctions/>.

[22] "In 2018, various changes were made to the exchange rate regime in the Bolivarian Republic of Venezuela, to unify the official exchange rate and make the foreign exchange market more flexible. As a result, a regime was created in which the exchange rate fluctuates as determined through auctions. The changes also made it possible to narrow the spread between the official and parallel exchange rates: from a multiple of 31.8 times at the end of 2017 to 2.8 at end-2018, and practically 1 in June 2019" (ECLAC 2019, p. 92; see also ECLAC 2018).

[23] This is how Strønen described the conditions in Venezuela during Maduro's administration: "Chávez is dead, the Maduro government has record-low support, the opposition has increased its electoral strength, the political conflict has hardened, the country's institutional weaknesses have become even more evident, oil prices have fallen drastically, the economy is in shambles, poverty levels have increased, social indicators have radically worsened, and many grass- roots activists have become de-mobilized. In short, Venezuela is a country in deep crisis. The international context is also different. The so-called Pink Tide is by most accounts and measures officially over. In its place, many predict the pendulum with swing toward a right-wing neoliberal model once more, as is already happening in Argentina and Brazil" (Strønen 2017, p.327–328).

References

Azzellini, D (2009) Venezuela's solidarity economy: collective ownership, expropriation, and workers' self-management. WorkingUSA: The Journal of Labor and Society, 12:171–1971
Baran P (1957) The political economy of growth. New York, Monthly Review Press
Bartley K, O'Brian D (2003) The revolution will not be televised (documentary). Los Angeles, Vitagraph Films
Chavez Frías H (2012) Golpe de Timón. I Consejo de Ministros del nuevo ciclo de la Revolución Bolivariana. Ediciones Correo del Orinoco, Caracas
Ciccariello-Maher G (2016) Building the commune. Radical democracy in Venezuela. Verso, London
Corrales J, Penfold M (2011) Dragon in the tropics. Brookings Institution Press, Washington
Curcio P (2016) The visible hand of the market. Economic warfare in Venezuela. Ministry of Foreign Affairs of Venezuela, Caracas
Dachevsky F, Kornblihtt J (2016) The reproduction and crisis of capitalism in Venezuela under Chavismo. Lat Am Perspect 44(1):78–93
Di John J (2009) From windfall to curse? Oil and industrialization in Venezuela, 1920 to the present. University Park, Pennsylvania University Press
Dieterich H (2005) Hugo Chávez y el socialismo del siglo XXI. Instituto Municipal de Publicaciones, Caracas
Economic Commission for Latin America and the Caribbean (2016) Economic survey of Latin America and the Caribbean. Santiago, ECLAC
Economic Commission for Latin America and the Caribbean (2018) Estudio Económico de América Latina y Caribe – República Bolivariana de Venezuela. ECLAC, Santiago. https://repositorio.cepal.org/bitstream/handle/11362/43964/105/EEE2018_Venezuela_es.pdf
Economic Commission for Latin America and the Caribbean (2019) Economic survey of Latin America and the Caribbean. Santiago, ECLAC
Enriquez L (2013) The paradoxes of Latin America's Pink Tyde: Venezuela and the project of agrarian reform. J Peasant Stud 40(4):611–638
Felicien A, Schiavoni CM, Romero L (2018) The politics of food in Venezuela. Mon Rev 70(2)
Gallegos R (2016) Crude nation. How oil riches ruined Venezuela. Lincoln, Potomac Books
Golinger E (2006) The Chávez code, cracking US intervention in Venezuela. Olive Branch Press, Nothampton
Hausmann R, Rodríguez F (eds) (2014) Venezuela before Chávez, anatomy of an economic collapse. The Pennsylvania State University
International Energy Agency (2019) Country Analysis Executive Summary: Venezuela. https://www.eia.gov/beta/international/analysis_includes/countries_long/Venezuela/venezuela_exe.pdf
Kovalik D (2019) The plot to overthrow Venezuela. Hot Books, New York
Moniz Bandeira LA (2016) A desordem mundial, o espectro total da dominação. Civilização Brasileira, Rio de Janeiro
Petróleos de Venezuela SA (2011) Consolidated financial statements. PDVSA, Caracas. Available on http://www.pdvsa.com
Petróleos de Venezuela SA (2016) Consolidated financial statements. PDVSA, Caracas. Available on http://www.pdvsa.com
República Bolivariana de Venezuela (1999) Constitución de La República Bolivariana de Venezuela. Gazeta Oficial, Caracas. Available on https://pdba.georgetown.edu/Constitutions/Venezuela/ven1999.html
República Bolivariana de Venezuela (2001b) Decreto con fuerza de ley de tierras y desarrollo agrario. Gazeta Oficial de la República, Caracas. Available on http://extwprlegs1.fao.org/docs/pdf/ven28661original.pdf
República Bolivariana de Venezuela (2006) Ley orgánica de hidrocarburos. Gazeta Oficial de la República, Caracas. Available on www.pdvsa.com

República Bolivariana de Venezuela (2007) Primer Plan Socialista de la Nación - Projeto Nacional Simón Bolívar. Gazeta Oficial de la República, Caracas. Available on http://www.psuv.org.ve/wp-content/uploads/2011/03/Proyecto-Nacional-Simón-Bol%C3%ADvar.pdf

República Bolivariana de Venezuela (2010) Ley de Tierras y Desarrollo Agrario. Gazeta Oficial de La República, Caracas. Available on http://extwprlegs1.fao.org/docs/pdf/ven183010.pdf

República Bolivariana de Venezuela (2012) Ley Orgánica del Trabajo de los Trabajadores y Trabajadoras (LOTTT). Gazeta Oficial de la República, Caracas. Available on https://oig.cepal.org/sites/default/files/2012_leyorgtrabajo_ven.pdf

República Bolivariana de Venezuela (2013) Ley del plan de la patria. Segundo plan socialista de desarrollo económico y social de la nación 2013-2019. Gazeta Oficial de la República, Caracas. Available on http://www.mppp.gob.ve/wp-content/uploads/2013/09/ley_plan_patria.pdf

República Bolivariana de Venezuela (2019) Linea del tiempo de la revolución bolivariana. Gazeta Oficial de la República, Caracas. Available on http://www.mppp.gob.ve

Robinson J (1979) Aspects of development and underdevelopment. Cambridge University Press, Cambridge

Salas Rodríguez L (2014) Escritos desde la guerra económica. Caracas, Fundación Editorial El Perro y la Rana

Strønen IA (2017) Grassroots politics and oil culture in Venezuela, the revolutionary petro- state. Palgrave Macmillan, London

Vasapollo L (2013) Tratado de métodos de análisis de los sistemas económicos, mundialización capitalista y crisis sistémica. Banco Central de Venezuela, Caracas

Weisbrot M (2015) Failed. What the 'experts' got wrong about the global economy. Oxford University Press, Oxford

White House (2019) Economic report of the president. Washington, DC. Available on https://www.whitehouse.gov/wp-content/uploads/2019/03/ERP-2019.pdf

Wilpert G (2007) Changing Venezuela by taking power. Verso, London

Yaffe H (2015) Venezuela: building a socialist communal economy? International Critical Thought, 5(1):23:41

Zahonero LA (2017) Chavismo. In: Moreiras A, Villacañas JL (eds) Conceptos fundamentales del pensamiento latinoamericano actual. Biblioteca Nueva, Madrid

Chapter 4
Economic Performance

4.1 Introduction[1]

This chapter makes an economic analysis of the Venezuelan economy between 1998 and 2018. It evaluates the economic policies applied by Chávez's and Maduro's administration, which were summarized in the last chapter. Particularly, the chapter investigates and tries to elucidate the evolution of the main economic and social parameters in the nation over the period, particularly in light of two questions: why did the Venezuelan economy show declining rates of economic growth over time? And what were the reasons for the severe crisis that occurred since the beginning of the second decade of the present century? The chapter argues that these behavior results from multiple causes. They involve the following ones:

1. Despite of the many social achievements of Chávez's administrations in Venezuela and the growth of the non-oil sector in the domestic economy, the macroeconomic policies did not drive the nation to a decoupling from the oil dependence; the adopted macroeconomic policies were marked by several problems, which will be detailed over the chapter, particularly as regards the stagnation of manufacturing and agriculture; as the economy still depended on oil exports and did not show structural changes toward higher stages of economic production, it was directly affected by the downward trend in oil exports which began in the world economy at the end of the 2000s under the impacts of the "subprime crisis" of 2008–2009.
2. The worsening of the economic scenario after 2013 was intensified by several additional changes in foreign oil markets, such as (i) lower prices and exported quantities after 2012, (ii) technical changes in the American markets leading to

[1] All statistical data can be accessed on the Internet. Regarding particularly the Venezuelan Central Bank and ECLAC, see www.bcv.gov.ve, "Estadísticas," and https://estadisticas.cepal.org/

© The Editor(s) (if applicable) and The Author(s), under exclusive license to Springer Nature Switzerland AG 2020

V. E. Schincariol, *Society and Economy in Venezuela*, SpringerBriefs in Sociology, https://doi.org/10.1007/978-3-030-60083-9_4

import-substitution in the United States, and then (iii) several sanctions applied by the United States to the Venezuelan economy.

3. The extreme drop in foreign reserves reached by 2015–2016 prevented the economy of operating under the old parameters; the subsequent low capacity to import, together with the drop in federal revenues led to fiscal and supply crises; these partially explain the rise in inflation rates, because of the supply shortages coupled with government's resorts to pure monetary expansion in order to face the crisis and pay its obligations. The behavior of large fractions of the private sector was also responsible for the worsening of the inflation rates and the very economic performance over Maduro's first term, in the form of speculation, planned disinvestments, capital flight, and other types of economic opposition. The recession, therefore, was a complex event that can only be understood in light of the interrelation of several variables: dropping exports, supply shortages, economic opposition, sanctions, and the subsequent negative effects of the high inflation on the economy as a whole.

4.2 Macroeconomic Aggregates and Sectoral Allocation

Figure 4.1 shows the Venezuela's Central Bank estimation of the size of the oil and non-oil sectors regarding the economy as a whole. According to this definition,[2] the relation of the oil sector to the economy as a whole dropped from 20% to 14% between 2003 and 2017. This path can apparently be regarded as a partial achievement of the economic plans since 2003 – that is, a lower dependence of the economy on the oil sector, or a higher growth of the other non-oil sectors. In official terms, the oil sector of the economy amounted to more than 20% between 1999 and 2005, falling to less than 15% after then, this fall being more intense after 2008. There seems to be four main periods regarding the relation between the oil and non-oil sector in Venezuela since 1999: (a) 1997–2003, non-oil GDP drops together with a more or less stable performance for the oil-sector; (b) 2004–2009, non-oil GDP increases, while oil-GDP still drops; (c) 2009–2013, there is partial recovery of both sectors and higher rates of growth of the non-oil sectors; and (d) 2014–2018, both sectors drop together with intense velocity, the fall of the oil-sector sector beginning 1 year before.

The problem with this division between oil and non-oil sectors is that a relatively high share of the alleged non-oil sector had as its main source of resources the oil sector. These oil resources were channeled to the "non-oil" sector directly in the form of wages and profits, PDVSA's local investments and purchases, and indirectly in the form of public social spending, state enterprises, or subsidies. All these sources of expenditures create domestic "Keynesian" multipliers, which are lowered by the high propensity to import of the economy (more of it in a moment). It is

[2] See BCV, Table 5.2.7, "Oferta y demanda global, a precios constantes de 1997 - Bolívares."

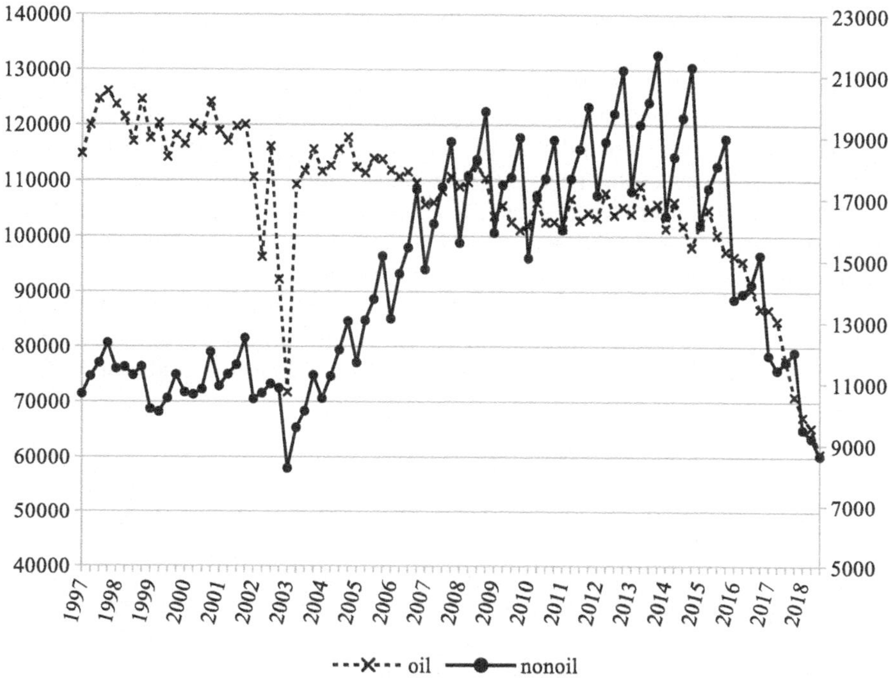

Fig. 4.1 Venezuela. GDP. Oil-sector (right axis) and non-oil sectors (left axis) in constant *Bolívares* (1997). 1997–2017. (Source: CBV, Table 5.2.7, "Oferta y demanda global, a precios constantes de 1997 – Bolívares")

very difficult to estimate these relations in exact figures, but it is important to note that all the economy is affected directly or indirectly by the behavior of those direct and indirect expenditures arising from PDVSA and the other authorized firms in the mining sectors.

In any case, the enduring dependence of the economy on oil exports can be seen more clearly by observing the joint performance of the oil sector and the non-oil sector when the changes in oil prices began to drop in international markets since 2011. The long-run trend seemed to point toward a relative diversification of the economy, though a limited one. But as soon as the oil sector drops more fiercely in 2014 (being the independent variable for the economy, in large measure), the non-oil sector followed suit.

In fact, the high growth of the non-oil GDP sector since 2002 seemed to profit partially from the previous high idle capacity in the overall economy before Chávez's first election. At the same time, Chávez's first administration benefited from better prices and higher exports for oil between 2002 and 2005 (both rising more than production), state's role growing in several ways (social policies, subsidies, nationalizations, new enterprises). As prices and export values went ahead of physical production until 2008, PDVSA's direct expenditures and state secondary expenditures financed by PDVSA exerted a natural multiplier effect on the domestic economy, leading to a high growth of the non-oil sector until 2011. However, as prices, exports, and physical quantity of oil all contracted, this source of aggregate demand was also diminished, and the economy as whole suffered the impacts of falling exports, rates of growth decreasing since 2011 (absolute decrease since 2014).

Table 4.1 shows a compilation of macroeconomic data furnished by several sources, which covers the 1998–2017 interlude. Some of them do not cover the entire period; therefore, some statistical series may complement each other. There were some discrepancies between the gross capital formation as informed by the Central Bank and Cepal-Stat, so both of them are showed.

The gross capital formation showed a U-shape path between 1998 and 2005 (or 2007); there was a decline in investments since 1998, which reached the original levels only by 2008 (around 30% of the GDP according to Cepal-Stat, or 37%

Table 4.1 Venezuela. Macroeconomic data (% of GDP). 1998–2017

	National savings [1]	Consumption [2]	GCF [1]	GCF [2]	Taxes [1]	Compensation of employees [1]	Profits (operating surplus) [1]
1998	18.0	53.0	30.0	26.0	11.0	40.0	51.0
1999	22.0	54.0	25.0	24.0	9.0	39.0	52.0
2000	27.0	56.0	24.0	25.0	8.0	35.0	57.0
2001	22.0	57.0	27.0	26.0	9.0	38.0	55.0
2002	23.0	58.0	21.0	23.0	9.0	36.0	57.0
2003	23.0	57.0	15.0	18.0	10.0	34.0	61.0
2004	30.0	58.0	22.0	22.0	11.0	32.0	60.0
2005	35.0	62.0	23.0	26.0	11.0	30.0	61.0
2006	35.0	65.0	27.0	32.0	12.0	32.0	58.0
2007	30.0	69.0	30.0	37.0	10.0	34.0	55.0
2008	31.0	68.0	27.0	38.0	11.0	32.0	58.0
2009	16.0	68.0	26.0	33.0	11.0	37.0	53.0
2010	25.0	68.0	22.0	32.0	10.0	32.0	60.0
2011	24.0	68.0	23.0	34.0	11.0	32.0	60.0
2012	19.0	69.0	27.0	43.0	11.0	35.0	57.0
2013	N.A.	73.0	19.6 [4]	36.0	N.A.	N.A.	N.A.
2014	N.A.	72.0	17.0 [4]	33.0	N.A.	N.A.	N.A.
2015	N.A.	70.0	14.4 [4]	24.0	12.0 [3]	24.0 [3]	50.0 [3]
2016	N.A.	69.0	9.5 [4]	17.0	10.0 [3]	22.0 [3]	48.0 [3]
2017	N.A.	68.0	6.2 [4]	9.0	10.0 [3]	18.0 [3]	49.0 [3]

Sources: estimated by the author using Cepal-Stat, "Main national accounts aggregates at current prices in national currency (% of the GDP)" [1], Central Bank of Venezuela, "Oferta y Demanda Global a Precios Constantes de 1997 – Bolívares" [2], '7.1.10, 'Cuentas Consolidadas de la Nación - base 1997 - Bolívares' (December) [3], and ECLAC 2019 [4]

according to the CBV); final private consumption expenditures (according to the CBV) were *increased* in relative terms since 1999, from 53% to 69% of the GDP by 2007. There was a relative growth in investments only between 2004 and 2008, the period during which exports showed the higher rates of growth; investments fall again after then. Following the 2008 crisis, both investments and savings dropped, savings being exceeded by investments in 2009 and 2012, and between 2015 and 2017, a path which boosted external debt. The crisis in oil exports after 2008 and then the crisis in the domestic economy itself led to a dramatic fall in the investment rate after 2013, the rate of gross capital formation in terms of GDP reaching only 14% in 2015 and 6% by the end of 2018 – an extremely low level under all standards. As Fig. 4.2 shows, government general expenditures increase from 15% to 23% of the GDP. This resulted both from the shrinking of the private sector of the economy as well as the rise in subsidies and monetization of the public expenditures particularly during Maduro's first term. As the economy plunged into crisis and investments disappeared after 2014–2015, domestic savings also fell, an increase in the foreign debt beginning since 2015.

These data suggests that the formation of savings was directly related to the performance of the foreign trade and also domestic investments; these later were not increased in relevant terms even after the strikes in PDVSA. As final private consumption expenditures showed a clear relative growth in parallel with a relative *drop* in compensation of employees, the gap between final private consumption and wages were filled by rising profits, whose share of the GDP reached 51% by 1998 and 60% in 2004 (wages dropped from 40% to 32% over the same period). Profits

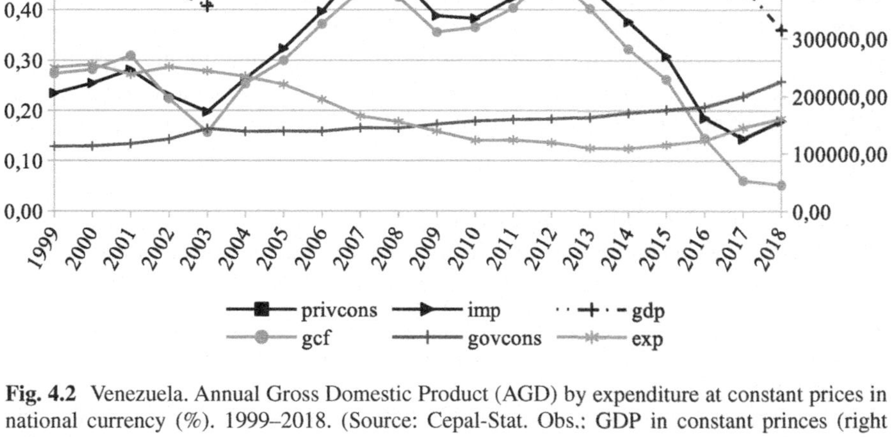

Fig. 4.2 Venezuela. Annual Gross Domestic Product (AGD) by expenditure at constant prices in national currency (%). 1999–2018. (Source: Cepal-Stat. Obs.: GDP in constant princes (right axis))

showed a relative increase over time, including after the new intense drop in real wages after 2012. This is an important feature: if wages were exceeded by profits while the rate of investments did not grow over the period, there was a clear waste of resources that, under conditions of forced accumulation, could have been used to boost investment capacities.

The data also suggests that the high inflation rates after 2014 penalized mainly the workers, Maduro's administration not being able to maintain a "fair division" of the domestic wealth between wage earners and employers, despite the nominal wage increases granted by the government. This forced savings, however, was again not used to maintain a reasonable rate of investments because, first of all, it was dropping significantly in absolute terms, reaching negative levels since 2005, together with the GDP itself. With regard particularly to the 2015–2018 period, the available data refers to Central Bank's "Cuentas Consolidadas de la Nación - base 1997, Bolívares" (table 7.1.10). These data show (1) extreme low and stagnated gross formation of capital (6% of the GDP[3]), which, however, exceeded the also extreme low levels of domestic savings; (2) after that 2015, negative rates of domestic savings now financed by more foreign loans; (3) wages decreasing from 24% to 18% and profits from 50% to 49% of the GDP; and (4) the sum of profits and mixed incomes (*ingreso mixto, neto*) rising from 65% to 70% of the national income. All these numbers translate the negative effects of inflation on workers' incomes; the government's failure in increasing minimum wages (despite of the official statements and some concrete measures, as nominal limits to profits); and an apparent growth in informal labor.[4]

Taxes in terms of the GDP showed an apparent stability and a small share in terms of the GDP since Chávez's first administration (maximum of 11%); however, these figures, which seemed to be confirmed by the CBV's own information for the 2015–2017 period, are significantly different from another source of information regarding this topic, which shows that total revenues *and grants* had an almost two-fold increase between 1999 and 2014, from 18% to 33%.[5] There is a clear difference between these two sources, and it seems that when grants are added to total taxes, their share in terms of the GDP has in fact shown a steady growth over time. It is more reasonable to assume that total taxes and revenues were in fact increased in light of the growing obligations of the government over time; in any case, the tax system and the public finance, from which PDVSA was a central element but not the only one, continued to show many problems that could be solved only by means of

[3] "Enfoque demanda," line B.1.b. ("demand approach")

[4] Sutherland, which cannot be considered a conservative critic, observed in a pessimistic vein: "The Bolivarian process can be best considered as a variant of the 'dependence of oil rents' [*rentismo petrolero*] which was already tested during the administration of Carlos Andrés Pérez (1974–1979). The ideological component and some anti-imperialist discourses confuse the majority of the analysts who study the president's declarations and not his concrete measures" (Sutherland 2018, p. 150).

[5] See Cepal-Stat, "Government operations (economic classification) as a percentage of the GDP, 1990–2014, Revenues and grants" and also Table 4.7.

"unpopular" and resolute measures. Some of these problems involved extremely cheap gasoline prices; overvalued exchange rates, which – beyond damaging local production – lowered prices for imports but resulted in less profits for the Central Bank and PDVSA when selling of dollars to the private market[6]; nationalizations of obsolete firms; cheap credit under negative real interest rates, damaging national savings; and high salaries in the public sector (for a discussion of some of these problems, see Sutherland 2018).

Figure 4.2 shows Venezuela's annual gross domestic product by *types of expenditure* for the 1999–2018 period – another source for macroeconomic aspects of the economy such as furnished by the Cepal-Stat. Although some minor numerical discrepancies in the data regarding the abovementioned sources, these figures give us additional insights regarding the macroeconomic performance of the economy over the period.

The relative share of private consumption showed a constant increase since the beginning, rising over the whole period in relative terms (from 55% of the GDP to 73% between 1999 and 2014). Results partially differ from Table 4.1, particularly with regard to the peak in investments in terms of the GDP (30%, 38%, or 40% by 2007–2008?), although the showed path is the same: gross capital formation showed an absolute increase between 1999 and 2001, but the economy then suffered the direct and indirect impacts of (i) the American crisis in 2001 on oil exports and then (ii) the strikes in PDVSA, both reducing the gross capital formation to approximately 15%–18% of the GDP. Also because of the previous high idle capacity created by the crisis, investments resumed quickly and faster than consumption after 2002, under a new boom in oil exports; but absolute investments were followed closely by imports and *also* by private consumption. In any case, this was the only period when investments grew faster than consumption. By 2007, a new deceleration began, investments and imports decreasing in relative terms; private consumption, however, stagnated around 68–70% of the GDP, instead of dropping. By 2010 investments briefly recovered, until 2012; but they went down again in parallel with imports, as private consumption reached around 73% of the GDP by 2013. Investments showed an erratic performance, and private consumption was never reduced. The government consumption almost doubled over the period, and since 2001 exports constantly dropped in relative terms until 2015.

According to Fig. 4.2, capital formation was related to imports over the whole period, suggesting the ongoing dependence of imported goods to maintain local production. Both imports and investments sink with incredible velocity after 2013, under the new impacts of the changes in foreign oil markets (lower prices, lower physical production, and then American embargoes). After reaching the maximum

---

[6] Particularly the foreign ones, who benefited from the overvaluation of the domestic currency vis-à-vis the dollar; "[t]he preferred mode of appropriation of the petroleum rent was not state financing of industry or infrastructure but rather the overvalued exchange rate, the principal beneficiary of which was foreign capital. While overvaluation of the bolivar expanded purchasing power abroad, it also fostered dollar flight and generated restrictions on its sustainability over time" (Dachevsky and Kornblihtt 2016, p. 12).

of 29% of the GDP by 2002, exports fade without stop, reaching only 12% by 2014. This performance in exports partially reflected the higher relative economic growth of the domestic non-oil sectors, as already mentioned, but also partially reflected the rising difficulties of the oil markets abroad, the economy facing an impasse by 2014. The performance of the gross capital formation and the GDP over the whole period (see figure 3.1), despite the nominal drop of exports in terms of the GDP. This partially reflected the higher prices for oil between 2002 and 2013 (excluding 2008–2009): higher prices allowed for higher gains per physical unit of production, which were partially redistributed from PDVSA to the non-oil sectors (see Fig. 4.6.). By its turn, as gross capital formation was always followed by imports, it can be also suggested that there was a permanent dependent relation between investments and the foreign supply of goods, showing a high propensity to import. This occurred partially because the decreasing share of the manufacturing production as regards the GDP.

In short, two conclusions arise from these data: (i) the behavior of the rate of investments was erratic and stimulated in broad terms by the exports, relying on imports to take place in material terms; (ii) there was not a meaningful reduction in private consumption so as to finance local investments with domestic resources.

Table 4.2 shows the Venezuelan main economic sectors as a share of the gross domestic product since 2002.

According to the official data, there was a quick relative growth of the non-oil and state sectors in the economy, particularly since 2003 for the former and 2013 for the latter. According to Central Bank's table 5.2.1, state sectors as a whole amounted to 25% of the total GDP in 2006 and 30% in 2013.[7] This was, in fact, one of the assumed goals of the administrations, that is, spreading state-owned enterprises in many different economic sectors.[8] If we accept the definition that a socialist economy is one in which "agriculture and trade as well as industry were nationalized or controlled by the state" (Davis 2014, p. 141), Venezuela became "more" socialist over time, but this was a crude simplification, because the private sector remained and was capable of exerting a strong influence on the overall economic conditions, particularly in the supply of consumption goods.

Manufacturing sectors, correctly regarded by Chávez as a decisive tool for the growth strategy because of their capacity to disseminate good externalities and allow for higher exports (see Thirlwall 2002 for a theoretical approach), saw a decline in their share of the GDP, from 18% to less than 8% between 1997 and 2018. Electricity generation also performed badly, leading to constant energy rationing (partially due

[7] This according to CBV's Table 5.2.1, which defines a public and a private sector for the economy as whole. See CBV, Table 5.2.1, "Producto interno bruto a precios constantes de 1997, en Bolívares; sectores público y privado."

[8] Such as in agricultural supply and fertilizers (Agropatria and Fertinitro); aluminum, gold, and steel extraction and production (Alcasa, CGV, Sidor); banks (Banco Bicentenario; Banco de Venezuela; Banco Industrial de Venezuela); telephone services (Cantv); firearms (Cavim); electricity (Electricidad de Caracas); food distribution (Mercal and PDVAL); automobiles (MMC and Venirauto [joint venture between Venezuela and Iran]); shipbuilding (Ucocar); computers and desktops manufacturing (Vit C.A., joint venture between Venezuela and China)

Table 4.2 Venezuela. Economic sectors. 2002–2018. % of the GDP

Years	A	B	C	D	E	F	G	H	I	J	K	L	M	N	O	P
2018	12	80	0.4	7	3	1	4	3	14	3	9	6	23	4	1	8
2017	11	80	0.4	9	3	1	6	3	11	4	9	6	23	5	2	9
2016	11	80	0.2	10	3	5	7	3	9	5	9	7	20	4	4	9
2015	10	80	0.3	12	2	7	9	3	8	7	9	7	16	5	6	10
2014	9	79	0.3	13	2	8	10	3	7	8	9	7	15	6	7	11
2013	10	79	0.3	12	2	8	11	3	6	7	9	6	14	6	7	11
2012	10	78	0.4	13	2	8	10	4	6	6	9	6	14	6	6	12
2011	10	78	0.5	13	2	8	10	4	6	5	9	6	14	6	5	12
2010	11	78	0.5	14	2	7	10	4	6	4	9	6	14	6	4	12
2009	11	78	0.5	14	2	8	10	4	5	4	9	6	13	6	4	11
2008	11	77	0.5	14	2	8	11	4	5	5	9	6	12	6	4	12
2007	12	76	0.7	14	2	7	11	4	4	5	9	5	12	6	5	12
2006	12	76	0.7	16	2	7	11	4	4	5	9	6	12	6	5	12
2005	14	76	0.7	16	2	6	10	4	3	4	9	5	13	6	4	10
2004	17	74	0.8	16	2	5	9	3	3	3	9	5	14	6	3	10
2003	18	74	0.8	16	2	5	8	3	3	2	10	5	14	6	3	8
2002	15	77	0.8	15	2	8	8	3	3	2	11	5	15	7	2	8

Source: CBV, Table 5.2.4, "Producto Interno Bruto por clase de actividad económica a precios constantes de 1997 (Bolívares)"
A. Oil sector; B. non-oil sectors; C. mining; D. manufacturing; E. electricity and water supply; F. construction; G. trade and repairing; H. transports and stores; I. communications; J. financial institutions and insurance; K. real estate services and renting; L. non-profit community, social and personal services; M. services and products provided by central government; N. private agriculture, restaurants, private hotels, and other public activities; O. financial intermediation indirectly estimated; P. taxes

to sabotages, according to the government). It is understandable that after years of impoverishment, there were strong appeals to implement actions that boosted social services. Accordingly, services had better achievements, and this certainly brought positive consequences in terms of a higher general well-being through a diversified supply. But as they could not improve the quality of Venezuela's foreign trade, it could be argued that between 2003 and 2011, the nation saw a high domestic growth of non-productive sectors pushed by the state sector and so by oil exports, along with a stagnated productive capacity, here understood in Kalecki's terms (see Kalecki 1968).

The most important increase in state's overall role in the economy came after 2014, when the total participation of all state activities in the economy was increased from 32% to 48% of the GDP in 2018. Products and services provided by the central government (with the exclusion of the oil-sector) were increasingly used as a counter-cyclical tool during the crisis, as the rest of the economy contracted after 2013.[9] Surely, it is not clear if so high rates would be achieved had the economy a

[9] When dealing with this level of aggregation, however, it is difficult to identify which part of these services nominally provided by the government were translated into more useful services to the population – schools, hospitals – and which part of those services meant the continuation of the traditional bureaucracies and sinecures in the public sector (typical in all Latin American nations, Venezuela included) which do not aggregate in terms of a higher general well-being.

more stable path. However, as Furtado once observed, "*external vulnerability,* a reflexion of fluctuations in the prices of primary commodities on the world market, led several Latin American governments to assume growing responsibilities on the economic plane even before the 1929 crisis" (Furtado 1977, p. 242). Analogous conditions were brought by the 2008–2009 financial crisis and the crisis in oil markets since 2012–2013; so, the expansion of the state functions was introduced again as an obvious necessity.

On the other hand, this expansion of the state activities was also accompanied by high rates of growth in real estate, private trade, and construction activities. This explains why the terms of a "mixed" or "hybrid" economy were more suitable to the Venezuelan conditions, as private markets – controlled by many hostile and strong groups – still accounted for half of the economy by 2018.[10] Financial intermediation had a significant expansion particularly since 2013, reflecting the indirect effects of the high inflation and higher poverty rates. Social services showed stable shares; agriculture saw many problems related to supply capacity.

Agriculture shall be also briefly mentioned. Venezuela has a very rich geography and plenty of natural resources beyond oil, such as natural gas, iron, bauxite, coal, gold, and diamonds. The nation has many opportunities to fishing in coastal waters. There are four more or less defined regions in geographical terms: the Maracaibo lowlands (northwest); northern mountains (the Andes); the *Llanos*, that is, the Orinoco plains in its central region; and the Guiana highlands in the southeast. Despite some limitations regarding the complex nature of its soil and geography,[11] there is a great potential for agriculture, which is still not fully utilized. The *Llanos* and the Maracaibo lowlands can be used for expanding agriculture and stockbreeding. Venezuela has also a low rate of population density, which is around 28 inhabitants per square kilometer, much less than – say – Japan (336/km^2), China (136/km^2), or South Korea (488/km^2). This could at least partially prevent diminishing returns from a rise in the ratio of labor to land. However, expanding agriculture is always not an easy task, because of the complexities involved in the task.

In theoretical terms, if the economic policy fosters food imports by means of different kinds of subsidies, the relative prices will work against domestic production. If there is a cultural bias against working the land and/or low wages (in the farming sectors and/or urban population), people will not easily cultivate land. In the absence of insufficient conditions to sell the domestic production – for example, a lack of basic infrastructure in the form of roads or other types of transport, or harsh working

[10] "The current situation is one of dual power, where the government controls the state oil company PDVSA (Petroleum of Venezuela, S.A., and through it the oil industry), but beyond that, state ownership of economic resources, and productive activity itself, is limited" (Yaffe 2015, p. 28).

[11] Some of the main limitations involve landforms and high altitude in the Andean mountains and the Guiana Highlands; low fertility in many parts of the Central and Eastern *Llanos*; drainage limits in the Lake Maracaibo and also along the Orinoco river; logistical and practical difficulties involving the Amazon forest in the South; ecological protected areas; etc.; for a discussion see, for example, Jaimes et al. 2002.

conditions – this tendency will be still higher. In other words, the preconditions and mechanisms which can detain the tendency toward a high urbanization and low agrarian production, which lead to a diminishing agricultural production, involve many variables. State policies can deal with these forces by the introduction of (a) land reform to eliminate idle areas and to stimulate family farming[12]; (b) adequate financing and infrastructure[13]; (c) favorable relative prices and existing demand; (d) and under certain circumstances even compulsory mechanisms, such as limits to labor mobility.[14]

Chávez officially recognized the problems of the Venezuelan agriculture. He declared in 2006:

> One of the biggest difficulties we have is related to the infrastructure to support agricultural production. By 2006 the investment reached 188 billion Bolivars, a figure that seems very low to me. I ask the ministers of the respective area, the Minister of Agriculture, the Minister of Finance, the Permanent Finance Commission of the National Assembly, the governors of the agricultural states [...] to put a great effort in this infrastructure investment on a nation level; that is [we shall develop] irrigation systems, rural aqueducts, greenhouses, roads, electrification, transportation systems, storage systems, cooling. In all of this there are great difficulties. Of course. We had been assigned the role of being oil producers and nothing more. (Chávez Frías 2013 vol. III, p. 327)

Accordingly, the Venezuelan government recognized the necessity of improving agriculture in its development plans by means of a higher productivity, public financing, and land reform (see RBV 2001a, 2001c, 2007). According to the *Firts Socialist Plan of the Nation - National Project Simón Bolívar* (RBV 2007), "food sovereignty implies the country's control of the production capacity and distribution of a significant set of staple foods that provide a high proportion of nutritional requirements for the population" (RBV 2007, p. 23). The document emphasized the necessity of creating the so called social-economy enterprises (*empresas de economía social*) and state-enterprises to boost "food sovereignty" and to develop "non-oil basic industries" (RBV 2007, p. 26). It also mentioned the necessity of "consolidating the agrarian revolution," to "expropriate idle lands" or lands without

[12] "Perhaps the most inconsistent element between the Land Law and the current reality of agrarian property in Venezuela is continued presence of large-scale *latifundios*, deemed to be 'contrary to the social interest'" (Lubbock 2019, p. 8).

[13] "For those receiving land, the next most important resource they could receive would be credit" (Enriquez 2013, p. 623). This author also discuss how credit.

[14] "The USSR in the 1920s, China in the 1950s and Vietnam in the 1970s and 1980s all experienced large-scale unemployment [because of the influx of peasants to towns]. Both the USSR and China dealt with the problem by the use of administrative measures. In the USSR from 1933 to the late 1970s, the Soviet authorities prevented the excess rural population causing urban unemployment by administrative controls over the outflow of labour from the villages (depriving villagers of internal passports). This reflected, and enhanced, the position of the rural population as second-class citizens. In China urban unemployment resulting from the influx of peasants into the towns was a serious problem in the 1950s. [...] The use of sending down enabled China to avoid the massive disguised unemployment that characterises the urban agglomerations and shanty towns of many Third World countries" (Ellman 2014, p. 242).

unclear titles of property. The *General Lines of the Economic and Social Development Plan of the Nation, 2001–2007* (RBV 2001c) observed that "the demand for food requires a substantial increase in the productivity of the sector to cover the internal supply and even open the possibilities of exporting at competitive prices and comparable to the capacity to purchase the population" (RBV 2001c, p. 59). These perspectives were also contained in the *Plan Pátria* for 2013–2019 (RBV 2013), which aimed at "definitively eliminating large states" [*latifúndio*], as well as "promoting the rise of cultivated lands," fostering "inland waterway transports," "promoting electricity in the countryside," and many other self-declared intentions to promote agricultural incentives (see RBV 2013, p. 9).

However, detecting problems is easier than solving them, even with goodwill and a progressive legislation which facilitated land expropriations. Historically, even great social revolutions and their resulting radical changes regarding land property did not solve all problems of agriculture, vis-à-vis the previous land concentration in the hands of the aristocracy or capitalists. For example, one of the main weaknesses of the Soviet agriculture was the absence of material incentives for families sharing the *kolkhozes* and *sovkhozes*, with their large plots of land and equipment, and fixed state prices for production. This, together with a system of relatives prices that stimulated heavy industrialization for many years, led to falling production, emigration, and demoralization (for a discussion see Ellman 2014). This was not the Chinese case after Deng Xiaoping (1980 onwards), when land was (re)distributed between families or smaller groups, who gained the freedom to sell their surplus production under market prices (see Bernstein 2010). This is the core of the Chinese agrarian policies up to now.

It is beyond our capacities to analyze in detail the performance of the Venezuelan agriculture over the period, which has attracted much attention particularly in the form of case studies, agriculture, and land reform being specific research problems in themselves (for a discussion of the Venezuelan agriculture land reforms, see, for example, Lavelle 2013; Enriquez 2013; Purcell 2013; Felicien et al. 2018; Lubbock 2019). There are also problems with adequate statistical data regarding the sector since at least 2016, including financial ones (for these difficulties see, for example, PROVEA 2019). Only a general trend regarding production will be traced here.

Despite the realistic characterizations and noble intentions of the Venezuelan government regarding the land question, which included land distributions, facilitated settlement,[15] as well as abundant credit,[16] there was not a sufficient perfor-

[15] "The agriculture ministry has reported that between 2003 and 2011 the government recovered 5753.264 hectares, and regularized 5859.087 hectares (PROVEA, 2019)" (Lavelle 2013, p. 142).

[16] After studying the impacts and the implementation of the land reform in Merida, Enriquez concluded that "there was an abundance of resources that could be invested in agricultural production; [...] a decision had been made to shower the countryside with credit; and that there might not be enough control over credit disbursement. (…) The multiplicity of institutions providing agricultural credit could be confusing for agrarian reform beneficiaries. It also opened up the possibility of an individual farmer or cooperative turning to a new institution each time a loan was defaulted on or not paid back in full" (Enriquez 2013, p. 623).

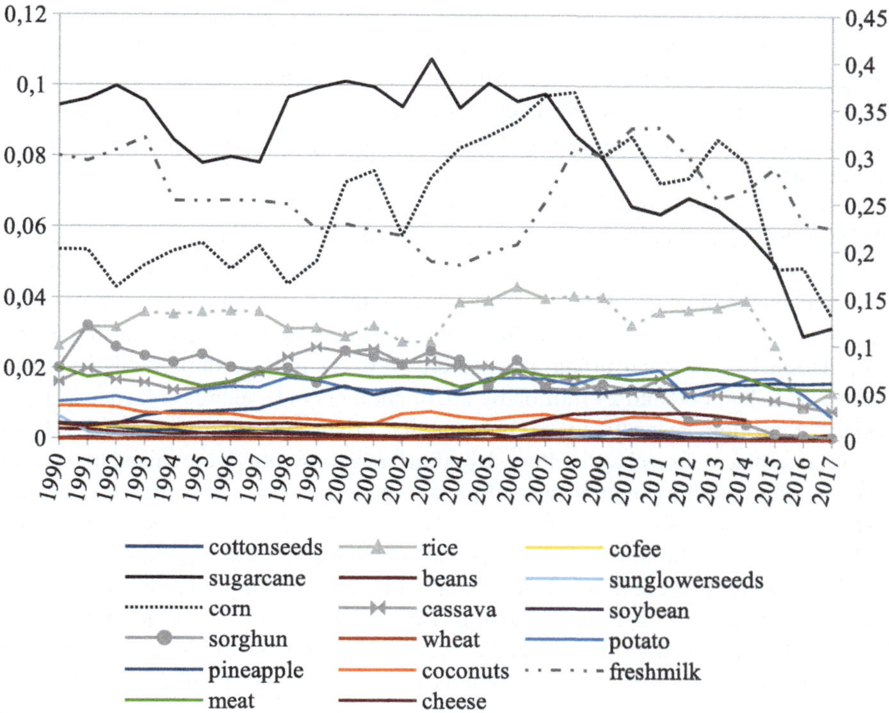

Fig. 4.3 Venezuela. Agriculture. Production of selected goods divided by the total population. 1990–2017. (Source: author's estimation based on data furnished by Cepal-Stat. Obs.: sugarcane in the right axis)

mance of the agrarian production on a per capita basis. The available statistical data suggests that production rates showed irregular and/or even declining paths. Regarding total agricultural area, total arable land reached 21.5 million hectares in 2003, this amount never changing after 2003. Permanent crops stagnated on 700 thousands hectares since 2003; the same for permanent meadows and pastures (18.2 million hectares since 2006). Irrigated area grew by 1.6 times between 2003 and 2008, a reasonable result indeed, but then stagnated.[17] Figure 4.3 plots the results for agriculture and stockbreeding for the 1990–2017 period in per capita terms (total production divided by the total Venezuelan population). In fact, despite all the successes and social benefits of the land reforms over the period,[18] overall results for production were very irregular between 2008 and 1998 and critical between 2017 and 2018. Sugarcane and corn showed clear rising patterns after 1997, a stable path until 2005, and a drop after 2008; the same occurred with fresh milk after 2010. The production of rice in per capita terms declined between 1996 and 2003 and then

[17] See "Cepal-Stat, Venezuela, Irrigated area" and "Agricultural area."

[18] Based on official figures, Enriquez observed that "between 2001 and 2010, 5.5 million hectares of land were confiscated from private owners," another very reasonable achievement; see Enriquez 2013, p. 622.

recovered and stabilized until 2014. After this year, rice growing suffered a major drop, as well as with sugarcane, corn, and milk. The cultivation of coffee, cassava, sorghum, wheat, potato, coconuts, and meat production all *dropped* in per capita terms between 2008 and 1998 and even more between 2017 and 2008. And with the exception of pineapple, all types of growing and/or production plummet between 20,008 and 2017.

It is beyond our capacities here to deal with the details of the agrarian policies in Venezuela; we can only mention some of the main likely reasons for that performance. Firstly, despite the official incentives to rural migration through several mechanisms,[19] there were no limits to labor mobility; therefore urbanization rates continued to grow. According to the data furnished by the Cepal-Stat regarding population by rural and urban areas, there were 21 million individuals living in urban areas by 2000 and 29 million by 2020; numbers in rural areas reached 2.9 and only 3.1 million, respectively.[20] Theoretically, urban agriculture could have been boosted in place of rural agriculture. But if urbanization rates were raised in parallel with declining employment in agriculture as whole (i.e., rural *and* urban agriculture, which jointly dropped from 10% in 2000 to 7.9% in 2011), it can be inferred that urban agriculture did not act as an eventual substitute for rural agriculture.

There were also conflicts in the countryside, as expropriations triggered resistance and conflicts (see Lavelle 2013, p. 149). Acting under constitutional mechanisms, the government has never achieved a complete achievement in land distribution because landowners were not defeated as a class. Land distribution also involved know-how, logistics, adaptation, financing, and obviously markets. The economic policies could also not solve all of these tasks by mere legislation, credit, and moral incentives. These mechanisms were limited after the deterioration of fiscal conditions after 2008 (see Table 4.7), as well as by the introduction of the "preferential dollar" exchange rate system in 2009 (at the cost of 2.6 *Bolívares Fuertes* per one dollar). The power of the old food import system was also not erased.[21]

[19] "[R]epeasantization" – through agrarian cooperatives and state-led expropriations of latifundias – emerged as a way to combat poverty and social exclusion and stimulate urban deconcentration. Through the Ministerio del Poder Popular para la Agricultura y Tierras (Ministry of Popular Power for Agriculture and Land), "the Venezuelan government has facilitated migration back to the countryside from the country's overpopulated urban centers" (Purcell 2013, p. 153). This work, based on case studies, carries out a broad discussion of the limits to land reform and their relation with the overall economic conditions. Lubbock also observed that "state's *Vuelta al Campo* (Return to the Countryside) campaign, and the creation of small-scale cooperatives (*Fundos Zamoranos*) between 2003 and 2006 [were created] in response to both hyper-urbanisation and peasant pressures for land redistribution" (Lubbock 2019, p. 11).

[20] See Cepal-Stat, Venezuela, "Population by rural and urban areas by sex."

[21] Felicien, Schiavoni and Romero also observed that: "[w]hile some important inroads were made in connecting the two initiatives [of agrarian reform and food security programs], the Chávez years saw no lasting rupture in the historic power of those who controlled the agrifood system. Thus, more food programs for the poor meant more food imports, which further consolidated the import complex, reinforced through multiple mechanisms of the state. Among these mechanisms was the granting of dollars from oil revenues to private enterprises, at highly subsidized rates, for imports of food and other goods deemed essential. This means that over the course of the Bolivarian

Lubbock observed that "[i]ndeed, after 2011, in the face of falling production in the countryside, Chávez's *Gran Misión AgroVenezuela* aimed to expand the total surface area under production, increase production of the main staple crops (corn and rice), and promote urban agriculture" (Lubbock 2019, p. 9). While this seemed to boost rice production between 2012 and 2015, and corn production between 2012 and 2014, both also dropped sharply after then.

According to Cepal-Stat, extreme poverty in the nation, which reached only 4.8% of the population, reached 9.1% by 2013 and 11.9% in 2014.[22] In light of the worsening social conditions (including famine?), it could be suggested that land reform and labor allocation should have been boosted by means of more resolute methods, particularly after the crisis in the balance of payments (firstly in 2009, and then from 2013 onward). This would have been a response to the falling foreign reserves, inflation, and food insecurity (which included the dependence on imports and speculation), in line with the functioning of an eventually new "import substitution" process.[23] However, the opposite has passed: as the economy contracted, the domestic production of food followed the lower aggregate demand and lower credit; subsidies for the import of basic goods were introduced; and the growing scarcity of foreign reserves – with the corresponding dropping supply of food imports which it brought – led to speculation with physical stocks. Thus, despite several local examples of successful experiments involving land reform, food sovereignty as a whole was still more damaged, and import dependence was intensified on a per capita basis. Additionally, the drop in the overall agricultural production per head also meant that less surplus production could be eventually channeled to exports.

A correlated feature of the structural performance of the nation is related to the share of employment of each economic sector over time. An eventual comparison

Revolution, state funds, while going toward many social programs, have also flowed into the private food import complex, amounting to major subsidies for the most powerful companies. The direct and indirect beneficiaries of this system have little incentive to alter it" (Felicien et al. 2018, p. 7).

[22] See Cepal-Stat, Venezuela, "Population living in extreme poverty and poverty by age, sex and geographical area."

[23] China also faced hyperinflation after the revolution (1949–1950), but with success, by means of a full land reform and the anchoring value in staple-grains. "First, peasants who had land distributed to them returned to work in the traditional self-sufficient economy. That meant that 88% of the population was immune to modern economic crises in cities, and that the government could focus its attention on the cities to deal with them. [...] Second, due to the accomplishment of the land revolution, the state succeeded in political mobilizing almost all the peasants, which supported the policy of supply-based value anchoring of the fiscal and financial system. [...] The most important function of land reform lay in the reduction of transaction costs when collecting surplus staple grains from self-sufficient and geographically scattered peasants. In the name of revolution, it became relatively easy for the state to tax and to purchase supplies from villages. Whether the state managed to collect enough staple grains and supplies was vital to its success in curbing speculation and hyperinflation" (Erebus et al. 2020). It is obvious that conditions were very different from modern Venezuela. The point here is to suggest how difficult can be to solve hyperinflation under conditions of high urbanization coupled with oligopolistic control of supply.

Table 4.3 Venezuela. Agriculture. Production of selected goods divided by the total population: relation between thousands of tons divided by total population between 2008–1998 and 2017–2008

	2008–1998	2017–2008
Cotton seeds	0.25	0.18
Rice	**1.30**	0.33
Coffee	0.90	0.58
Sugar cane	0.89	0.36
Beans	**1.29**	0.89
Sunflower seeds	**2.37**	0.12
Corn	**2.24**	0.36
Cassava	0.75	0.47
Soybean	**7.46**	0.14
Sorghum	0.70	0.05
Wheat	0.33	0.45
Potato	0.90	0.42
Pineapple	**1.19**	**1.21**
Coconuts	0.97	0.87
Milk	**1.25**	0.72
Meat	0.99	0.80
Cheese	**1.65**	N.A.

Source: author's estimation based on data furnished by Cepal-Stat

between the GDP by sector and the total employment in this sector would give the average productivity of each sector over time. The ECLAC estimated the share of the employment by economic sector in Venezuela over the period, such as shown by Table 4.4.

There was a general correspondence between the GDP and the employment structure over time in manufacturing and agriculture, both of them showing a declining rate of participation of employment as a share of the total employment. Both of these sectors saw a sharp drop during Maduro's administration, showing the intensity of the economic decline. By its turn, oil extraction as a share of the GDP has dropped since 1998, but despite being the sector with the higher product per head saw a relative increase in the total share of the national employment from 0.6% to only 1.4%. The rise is irrelevant for all practical purposes, this path being probably the result of a conscious allocation of the workforce for social or political reasons (to remedy the growing unemployment and to facilitate the political control of PDVSA, particularly).[24] Wages and salaries paid directly by the government showed a constant increase since Chávez's first administration (in terms of the GDP), more than doubling between 2000 and 2014, from 3.4 to almost 7%. The rise in the relative share of the public sector suggests that it was used as a means of ameliorating the rising unemployment particularly since 2013.[25]

[24] Ellner observed that "[s]ince 1998, PDVSA's workforce has more than tripled, from 40,000 to over 150,000" (Ellner 2017, p. 14).

[25] Presumably, public sector here means state administration.

Table 4.4 Venezuela. Employment by selected economic sectors (% of the GDP). 2000–2014

	Agriculture	Mining	Manufacturing	Electricity	Construction	Trade	Transports	Services	Other services	Nonspecified	Government
2000	10.6	0.6	13.3	0.6	8.3	25.8	6.8	4.9	29	0.1	3.7
2001	9.6	0.5	12.6	0.6	8.3	26.2	7	5	30	0.1	4.4
2002	9.9	0.5	11.7	0.5	7.9	26.8	7.3	4.9	30.2	0.3	4.2
2003	10.7	0.5	11.6	0.5	7.1	25.6	7.5	4.7	31.3	0.4	4.3
2004	10.4	0.6	11.3	0.5	7.6	24.2	8.2	4.8	31.1	1.4	3.9
2005	9.7	0.7	11.6	0.5	8	24.4	8.1	4.8	31.3	0.9	3.5
2006	9.1	0.7	12.2	0.5	9.5	23.6	8.2	5	31.1	0.2	3.8
2007	8.7	0.9	12.3	0.4	9.7	23.5	8.7	5.1	30.4	0.2	3.9
2008	8.5	0.9	11.9	0.5	9.7	23.7	8.8	5.2	30.6	0.2	4.1
2009	8.8	1	11.8	0.5	9.2	23.6	8.8	5.2	30.8	0.4	4.9
2010	8.7	1.1	11.5	0.5	8.9	23.4	9.2	5.5	30.7	0.3	5
2011	7.9	1.1	11.3	0.5	9	23.9	9.3	5.6	31.2	0.3	5.2
2012	7.7	1.3	10.8	0.5	8.6	24.5	9	5.5	31.8	0.3	5.8
2013	7.4	1.3	11.3	0.4	8.3	24.5	9.3	5.8	31.4	0.2	5.8
2014	7.9	1.4	11.7	0.4	8	24.1	9	5.7	31.6	0.2	6.9

Source: Cepal-Stat. For government, see Cepal-Stat, "Government operations (economic classification) as a percentage of GDP, 1990–2014"

Construction, trade, and transport also had an overall stability regarding their share of employment, which reinforces our statement that despite the falling relative share of the oil extraction in terms of the GDP since 1998, this diversification of the economy was not achieved by means of a stronger manufacturing and agricultural sectors, but by "unproductive" ones. As already mentioned, most of these sectors have their importance in terms of the developing "human capital," fostering economies of scale and expanding the housing provision, but they cannot per se increment the production of food and tangible goods, nor export the majority of their final services. These data regarding the relative shares of employment reinstate the abovementioned observations that the economy saw a declining participation of the oil sector and a higher diversification, but this was not translated in a better capacity to export and to raise the domestic production of tangible goods.

4.3 Balance of Payments and Oil Exports

The abovementioned features, particularly regarding the performances in manufacturing and agriculture, help to explain why the growth of the economy showed a high propensity to import since 2003. As already mentioned, the question of the pattern of imports is a decisive one regarding the processes of development (socialist or not). Figure 4.4 shows the structure of the total imports of Venezuela for the 1997–2018 period.

According to the ECLA (Cepal-Stat), the approximate total amount of the Venezuelan exports reached US$ 1.01 billion between 1998 and 2016; imports reached 60% of this value over the same period. Total imports as a share of the GDP showed a steady increase from 20% by 1999 to more than 50% in 2009; this share then dropped again, reaching only 20% by 2012 and 25% by 2017. The first stage is related to Venezuela's boom in oil exports and higher domestic growth; the second is related to the crisis in its balance of payments, which deepened after 2013 and prevented a rise in imports as a share of the GDP.

The imports of basic goods were increased after 1998, from 20% by 1999 to 35% of total imports in 2008. The share of basic goods dropped again after 2008, reaching 19% of total imports by 2014. The imports of intermediate goods showed a more or less stable path, ranging between 50% and 65% of total imports over the whole period; there was a relative drop for them after 2003, but a new upward movement until 2008. Imports related to non-oil gross capital formation more than doubled between 1999 and 2007 (from 10% of total imports to almost 30%), but showed since then a clear drop and a stagnation around 20% of total imports until 2014. There is a lack of information regarding them for the 2014–2018 interlude; apparently, the imports of capital goods reached 30% of the total (and reduced) imports by 2018. These data suggests that as domestic manufacturing dropped in terms of GDP over the period, in parallel with the growth of the several service sectors of the economy (see Table 4.2.), the bunk of these imports of capital goods was channeled

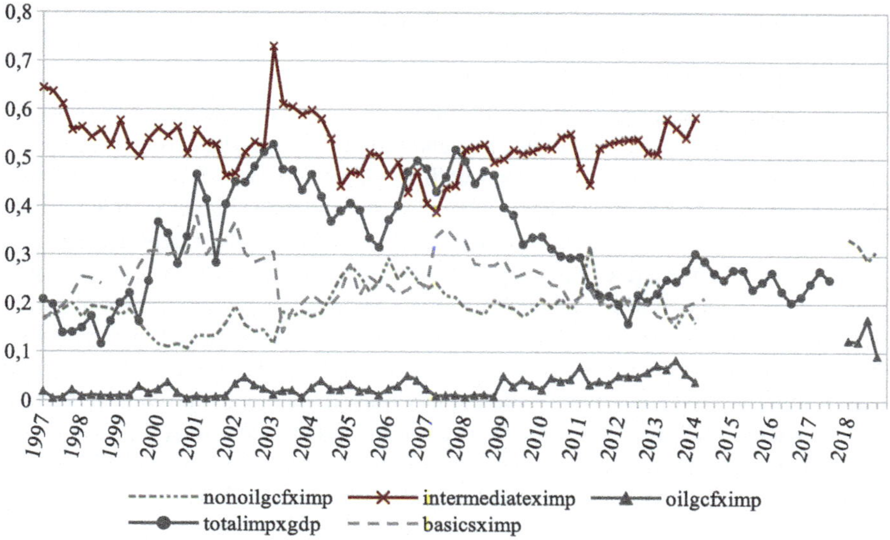

Fig. 4.4 Venezuela. Imports as a share of the GDP and imports by type as a share of total imports. 1997–2018 (or last available information). (Source: for total imports as a share of the GDP, see CBV, "Cuentas consolidadas de la nación, base 1997, en Bolívares"; for the others, CBV, "Importaciones de bienes FOB según sectores y destinos económicos de origen, en millones de US$." Obs.: disaggregated by imports of non-oil gross capital formation; intermediate goods; gross capital formation in oil sectors; basic goods; and total imports to the GDP)

mainly to "non-productive" sectors (according to our definition), along with a fast increase in basic goods imports between 1999 and 2008 and the ongoing dependence of intermediate goods. Regarding those goods related to gross capital formation in the oil sectors, they were marked by stability and a small share of total imports between 1999 and 2008, but since then they started to grow, reaching almost 20% of the total imports. This suggests that as gross capital formation related to the non-oil sectors dropped since 2008, the relative participation of the oil-sector in the rate of investments rose again, although both sectors contracted by approximately 40% between 2008 and 2014 (see Fig. 4.1.).

Despite the complexities involving the description of these figures, it is more or less clear that there was not a model of forced industrialization over the period 1999–2008, a relatively high share of foreign reserves being consumed by basic goods and the other one by the imports of capital goods used by the services sectors, given that manufacturing was not growing in relative terms. And as the share of manufacturing sectors dropped still more fiercely between 2009 and 2014 (from 14% to 7% of the GDP), the apparent relative rise in the import of capital goods not related to the oil sector seems to be more associated with an *absolute* drop in imports of basic goods; that is, this rise in the imports of capital goods cannot be attributed to a recovery in the domestic production, which was radically declining in absolute and relative terms.

If we compare the amount of imports per inhabitants in Venezuela with some of their Latin American counterparts, the high propensity to import in Venezuela over the period 2003–2009 becomes more clear.

Venezuela showed one of the highest rates of imports per head between in the region 2003–2008, in parallel with Chile and Mexico – which have free trade agreements and goods economic relations with the United States. Between 2002 and 2012, imports per head in Venezuela were almost three times higher than imports in Brazil and Argentina, which also enjoyed cyclical booms in their exports, reaching similar levels than in Chile. After 2012 the deceleration of imports in Venezuela was much more faster and intense than in the other nations, reaching the levels of Brazil for the first time by forced means (literally, a crisis in the balance of payments). Even with Venezuela's rate of GDP growth eventually surpassing the Brazilian and Argentinian ones, the fact that the potentially most dynamic and productive sectors in Venezuela – the manufacturing sectors – were growing less than the total economy shows that the rate of imports for consumption were significantly higher in Venezuela, in relative terms. Ecuador and Bolivia also depended heavily on commodities – crude oil and natural gas – but allowed for much less imports. In comparative terms, Chile and Mexico did not have to compress so much its imports because copper prices did not suffer so strong a reduction than oil.[26] In any case, had the administrations in Venezuela imposed more strict restrictions regarding the expenditure of foreign reserves since the 2000s, the economy would not have faced so acute a crisis in its balance of payments.

The second period regarding imports begins in 2008. The shocks of the international crisis, and then the crisis in oil markets (more of it in a moment), clearly drove the economy to a new situation, the boom initiated at the beginning of the 2000s having been finished. Basic goods drop and intermediate goods rise until 2014 (all in relative terms). There was a strong drop of total imports related to the GDP; that is, a strong drop in imports given a crisis in exports, which suggests the ongoing dependence of the domestic economy of the oil exports. Strictly speaking, Chávez's administrations had 10 years of a booming oil markets to implement development, that is, using the oil surplus to (1) implement social policies and (2) foster non-oil sectors. Even if we accept that these were sincere goals of his administration, it is clear that the resources achieved through oil exports were not successfully utilized.

The worsening of the conditions for the oil market since 2013 drove the economy to more falling reserves of hard currency and so to a growing physical impossibility of maintaining that type of growth, not to mention a deeper effort in import-substitution. Falling reserves translated the interruption of any virtual "socialist primitive accumulation" by means of the most important source of economic surplus in that moment, that is, oil exports. The crisis in oil markets interrupted the (modest) effort of diversification of the domestic economic growth stimulated by state, despite the slower path of manufacturing.

Table 4.5 shows results for the Venezuelan balance of payments since 1999.

[26] See Cepal-Stat, "Prices indexes of leading export commodities yearly."

Table 4.5 Venezuela. Balance of payments – selected transactions. 1999–2018. US$ millions

Years	Current account	Services	Income	Current transfers	Venezuelan FDI abroad	FDI in Venezuela	Portfolio assets	Portfolio liabilities	Net results
1999	2112	−2839	−1453	−67	−872	2890	248	1857	1068
2000	11,853	−3253	−1388	−170	−521	4701	−954	−2180	5935
2001	1983	−3305	−2020	−148	−204	3683	397	710	−1839
2002	7599	−2909	−2756	−157	−1026	782	−1354	−956	−4427
2003	11,796	−2634	−2337	20	−1318	2040	−823	−143	5443
2004	15,519	−3383	−3673	−72	−619	1483	−813	−1271	1900
2005	25,447	−3997	−2202	−62	−1167	2589	−2311	3246	5454
2006	26,462	−4410	−1045	−78	−1524	−508	−5966	−3983	4964
2007	13,464	−9112	515	−739	495	3288	458	4088	5742
2008	31,297	−11,067	−1567	−933	−1311	2627	4199	610	9275
2009	429	−11,181	−4646	−651	−2630	−983	4098	5372	−10,262
2010	5585	−12,460	−6208	−900	−2492	1574	888	3143	−8060
2011	16,342	−14,950	−9079	−801	370	5740	−60	2243	−4032
2012	2586	−17,238	−11,099	−1003	−4294	5973	−1275	4051	−996
2013	4604	−17,041	−8707	−1218	−752	2680	1363	−1955	−5490
2014	4919	−14,870	−7425	−207	−2373	−1028	2615	392	−718
2015	−16,051	−12,163	−7661	−155	−399	769	187	−3454	−4051
2016	−3870	−8159	−6918	174	−1041	1068	652	−1826	−6808
2017	8706	−6321	−7567	587	−2234	−68	826	−1235	−490
2018	6298	−6491	−7973	1951	−661	886	414	−46	955

Source: Cepal-Stat

From a realistic point of view, current account surpluses, boosted by oil exports, had significant increases only between 2002 and 2008. Since then, they declined and gave room to much lower results, including deficits in 2015–2016. Venezuela's overall balance relating services and primary and secondary income have been always in deficit, negative results growing until 2012, followed by lower values expressing the lower economic activity (which also affected the foreign enterprises). Negative results for the current transfers in the balance of payments traditionally expressed the high number of foreigners in Venezuela – approximately 1002 million by 2000 and 1357.7 million according to the United States by 2019 (see United Nations 2019), but much more according to the official declarations of the Venezuelan government. However, the emigration of Venezuelans after 2013–2014 helped to achieve positive results in current transfers for the 2016–2019 period, as more Venezuelans working abroad were sending resources to their families. According to the United Nations Population Division (United Nations 2019), total remittances from Venezuelans living abroad reached only US$ 17 million by 2000 but US$ 297 million in 2019. According to Cepal-Stat (Table 4.5), total current transfers reached positive values of US$ 174 million by 2016, US$ 587 million in 2017, and US$ 1951 million in 2018, although it is not possible to know if the majority of these values refer to emigrant's remittances in spite of international aid, donations, etc., as there is no detailed information on this issue in both RBV as well as ECLAC's sources (they only show results for total current transfers).

The growing negative results in income accounts express the relative freedom of Venezuelan residents (individuals as well as capitals) and foreign firms operating in Venezuela to export their profits, as well as debits in the form of portfolio investments, while foreign reserves were abundant[27]; these values reached very high levels after 2012 (an average of US$ 7 billion per year), erasing all current account surpluses over the period and largely exceeding the inflow of foreign direct investments. When regarding the net results of all external transactions of Venezuela, it can be seen that the strong rise in oil exports since the beginning of the 2000s, which reached US$ 98 billion by 2008 (see Table 3.1.), was almost completely lost not only in imports but also by international services and profits remittances. This relative freedom of exporting capital when reserves were available expressed one of the main differences between "Bolivarian socialism" and more centralized models.[28]

By 2009 the foreign enterprises panicked and profit remittances quickened, the deficit in the primary income account reaching US$ 11 billion in 2012. Foreign

---

[27] Lubbock observed: "Subsidising hard currency for domestic capital, in the absence of stronger state oversight, significantly undermined national development. With access to cheap foreign exchange, national capitals often engaged in a type of fraud in the form of overinvoicing, or importing empty containers. Despite capital controls, Venezuelan firms could stash their dollars abroad by merely buying bonds of foreign companies (in local *bolivares*), and reselling them on the New York Stock Exchange for dollars" (Lubbock 2019, p. 13).

[28] Yaffe observed that "conservative estimates calculate that the Venezuelan elite have deposited more than US$145 billion overseas between 2003 and 2012. The government's international foreign exchange reserves have fallen from US$12 billion in 1997 to US$3 billion in 2013" (Yaffe 2015, p. 29).

investment in oil-related activities (in the form of joint ventures with PDVSA) was also severely reduced over Chávez's administrations, being practically negative since 2013.[29] The overall negative balance in equities, investment funds, and other financial instruments more than doubled after 2012, reaching US$ -4.4 billion in 2018. Venezuela's investments abroad were partially decreased since 2012, as well as foreign investments, which reached US$ 6 billion in 2012 and only US$ 900 million in 2018, and null results for 2017. Portfolio assets were more or less stable between 2002 and 206, being increased between 2007 and 2014 (amounting to US$ 3 billion in 2014), and then contracted again. Total portfolio liabilities dropped rapidly after 2012, when they reached US$ 4 billion. The fall in (1) the Venezuelan investments abroad, as well as in the foreign investments in Venezuela and (2) the nation's decreasing assets and also liabilities (i.e., foreign loans and foreign direct investments in Venezuela[30]), cannot be dissociated from the increasing American sanctions since 2014, as well as the lower economic activity and uncertainty related to the political scenario.

As abovementioned, it is true that the economy saw a faster development of the non-oil sectors over Chávez's administrations, being reliable the official data on this issue. It does not mean, however, that Venezuela was free from its oil dependence, particularly to the United States. On the contrary, oil exports were still essential features of the economy by 2013, the domestic economic growth being still dependent on these resources. The 15 years of Chávez interventionist administrations were not sufficient to change the pattern of the Venezuelan exports, almost completely covered by oil exports (particularly crude oil). When the crisis in oil markets deepened, all the economy contracted.

As a matter of fact, oil sales are a complex result of the interconnection between three variables: (a) physical production and supply capacity; (b) prices per oil barrel; and (c) demand. In the Venezuelan case, variable (a) was reduced since 2004; variables (b) and (c) were reduced since 2011, all leading to deep consequences. Figure 4.5 shows changes in (i) oil prices, (ii) physical production of oil, and (iii) the total earnings of oil exports in Venezuela between 1998 and 2016. In the case of physical production, there was a (1) reduction in the physical supply since 2011, which did not have so strong impacts because of rising prices for oil until 2008, and (2) a reduction between 2009 and 2011 (Fig. 4.6).

Critics have argued that the "political" utilization of PDVSA's profits led to dire economic conditions for the enterprise, this being one of reasons of the economic crisis in the nation (see Corrales and Penfold 2011, Hausmann and Rodríguez 2014 and Gallegos 2016). This is a superficial assessment. It is true that, as it can be seen, the physical production of oil has been dropping since 2004 with a moderate but per-

[29] The article 9 of the Venezuelan Hydrocarbons Law (2006) states that extraction, transport, and storage of oil products shall be conducted by the Venezuelan State.

[30] "*Direct investment* is often referred to as an asset for the economy of the direct investor and as a liability for the economy in which the direct investment enterprise operates" (IMF 1993, p. 88). Thus, negative values means a net decrease in liabilities for the economy in which direct investments operates vis-à-vis its own direct investments abroad.

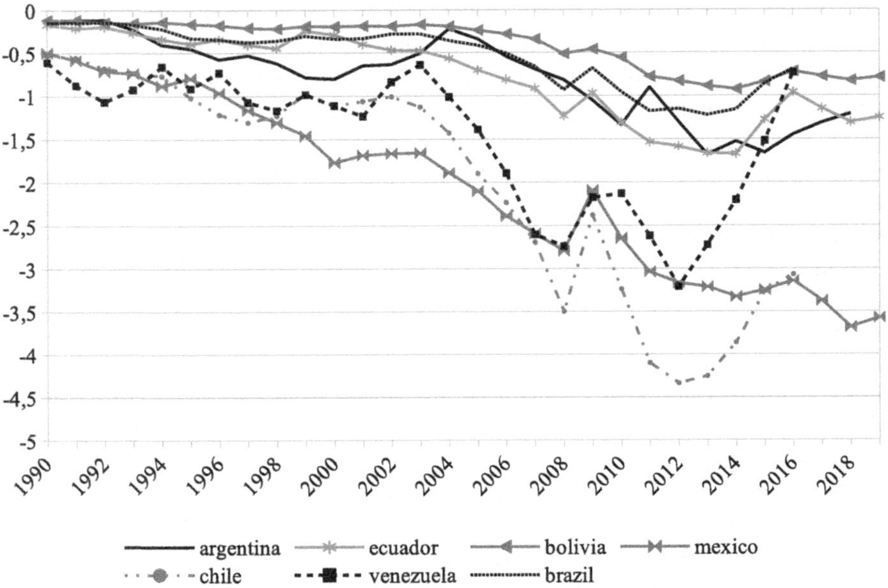

Fig. 4.5 Selected nations. Imports divided by total population. 1990–2019. (Source: author's estimation using data available on Cepal-Stat)

manent decrease. Given this performance, changes in total gains have been a direct function of changes in prices according to higher or lower demand. With given declining prices, a higher supply would bring higher losses by each unity of physical production; in this case, if prices covered costs with some net margin, some profits could still be made to a certain degree. Of course, with lower production and lower exports at the given prices, the economic losses would be exacerbated. But it is doubtful if a higher supply capacity should have been fostered under declining prices mixed with lower external demand, both of these variables not being controlled by PDVSA.[31]

This was the case since 2011, when lower prices were conjugated with ongoing *lower* external demand, particularly the American one. Price changes have been very unstable between 2003 and 2010, but since 2011, the fall in oil prices has no precedent in recent history, leading to the worst possible situation. Prices in 2016 were only 65% of prices in 2008, Venezuela's total exports (in US$ million) reaching approximately 30% in 2016 with regard to the values exported in 2008. Changes in exports fall behind changes in prices since 2012, showing also the difficulties in

[31] As Yergin observed, "Chávez made a decisive policy change that would reverberate throughout the world. Venezuela would no longer pursue a strategy of increasing revenues by increasing outputs. Indeed, it now became the strongest advocate in OPEC for cutting back on production and observing quotas" (Yergin 2011, p. 242). Obviously, this perspective assumed at least constant demand and more or less stable prices, which was not the case over the Venezuelan crisis. This partially explains the government's reluctance in devaluating the national currency in face of external prices; for a given falling external demand for oil, devaluation meant worsening terms of trade.

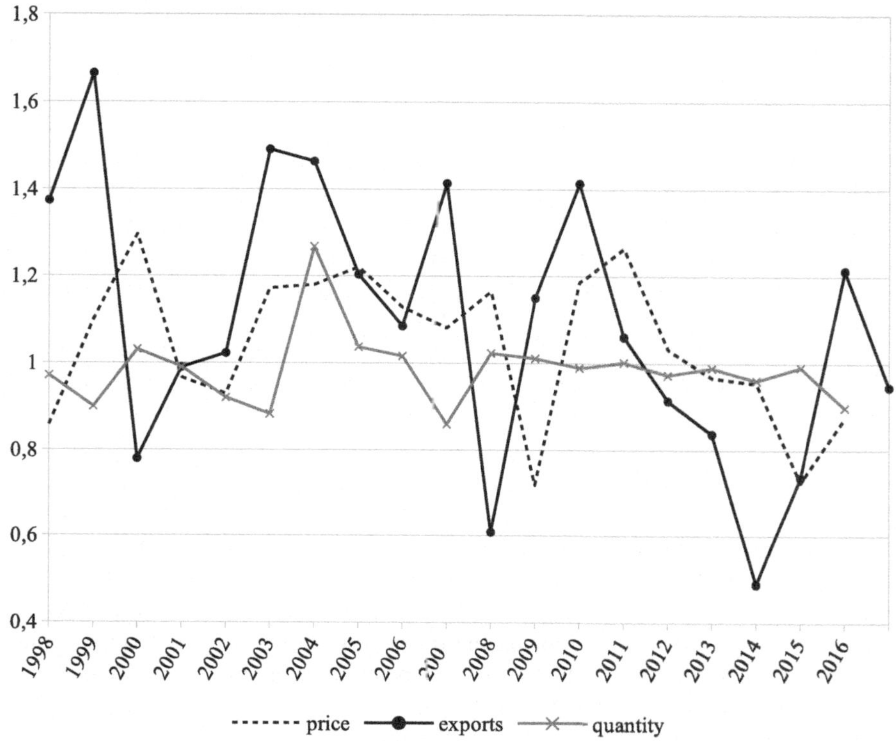

Fig. 4.6 Venezuela. Changes (t2/t1) in oil exports, oil prices, and oil production. 1997–2016. (Sources: for oil exports, CBV, "Exportaciones de bienes y servicios según sectores," US$ million; for prices, Cepal-Stat, "Índices de precios de los principales productos básicos de exportación anuales, ano base 2010=100"; for oil production per year (kilotonnes [kt]), IEA)

finding new buyers, as well as a saturated market in the United States, given (i) the introduction of the shale gas and related activities, (ii) the growing domestic oil production and the corresponding decline in oil imports, and then also (iii) sanctions against Venezuela since 2017.[32] Venezuelan total exports in 2016 reached only 16% of those made in 2008, which shows the dimension of the fall in exports, export gains falling faster than prices since 2010.

Table 4.5 shows PDVSA's main expenditures and net profits over 2011–2016 (last available results). There was a huge drop in revenues between 2013 and 2016. Purchases of oil and its by-products appear as the main costs, as PDVSA also distributes and refine domestic and imported oil (importing 65% of the total domestic oil supply in 2017; see IEA 2019b, p. 7). The table shows the approximate values for the resources of PDVSA which were used to finance social programs, subsidies,

[32] See "U.S. Imports by Country of Origin" and "U.S. Crude Oil Production" on https://www.eia.gov/dnav/pet/pet_crd_crpdn_adc_mbbl_m.htm and https://www.eia.gov/dnav/pet/pet_move_impcus_a2_nus_ep00_im0_mbbl_m.htm

Table 4.6 PDVSA. Costs, expenses and profits. US$ millions 2011–2016.

	1	2	3	3.1	4	4.1	5	5.1
Years	Revenues	Purchases of oil and other products	Contributions to social development	% of revenues	Income tax	% of revenues	Profits	% of revenues
2008	94,929	36,849	6923	7.0	3849	4.0	3164	3.0
2009	73,819	25,932	3514	4.0	3310	4.0	4394	5.0
2010	125,499	44,600	14,733	11.0	4280	3.0	9491	7.0
2011	125,519	39,783	30,079	24.0	2007	1.0	4447	4.0
2012	127,611	40,012	17,336	14.0	7279	5.0	5149	4.0
2013	134,326	37,017	13,023	10.0	7845	5.0	12,907	10.0
2014	101,552	37,266	5321	5.0	5106	5.0	9074	9.0
2015	55,539	22,965	9189	17.0	−3717	−6.0	7345	13.0
2016	41,977	17,817	977	2.0	817	1.0	828	2.0

Source: Consolidated Financial Statements 2010, 2011, and 2016 (PDVSA 2010, 2011 and 2016)

and investments in the rest of the economy between 2011 and 2016. These operations reached almost 25% before the economic crisis which began in 2013. They were lowered until 2016, to the point of being almost suspended. This policy led to the contradictory effects of adjusting the financial position of the enterprise while lowering state's budget related to social expenditures, as well as subsidies and investments. PDVSA was exempted from income tax in 2015 and partially in 2016, a decision which improved its profitability (Table 4.6).

The reduction of oil markets for Venezuela in the United States is the main variables behind this result; these difficulties would deepened by 2017 because of new financial sanctions against Venezuela and PDVSA taken by president Donald Trump (see introduction, footnote 2). According to the IEA, the United States imported 538.000 kt in crude oil by 2005; this quantity was severally reduced over time, reaching only 393.000 kt by 2017 (27% less). The United States also exported three times more natural gas over the period. By its turn Venezuela's physical production dropped more or less continuously and according to the same proportion, from 169.000 kt to 110.000 kt between 2005 and 2017 (35% less). As approximately 80% of the Venezuelan exports went to the United States in 2008, this quantity dropping to around 50% until the end of 2018, these changes in the American oil policies toward Venezuela should be considered as the main variable related to the worsening financial results of PDVSA.[33] Additionally, total world oil production grew by 10% between 2009 and 2016. Given that, what benefits could Venezuela achieve from a much higher supply capacity? It should instead focus on its refining capacities, so as to lower oil imports and exchange refined oil exports for crude oil.

Figure 4.7 shows the plotting of Venezuela's imports and exports together with its sales to the United States.

[33] By 2019, the IEA observed that "the United States [still were] the primary destination for Venezuelan crude oil shipments and receives about 41% of Venezuela's total exports" (IEA 2019a, p. 3), a statement also supported by Figure 5.

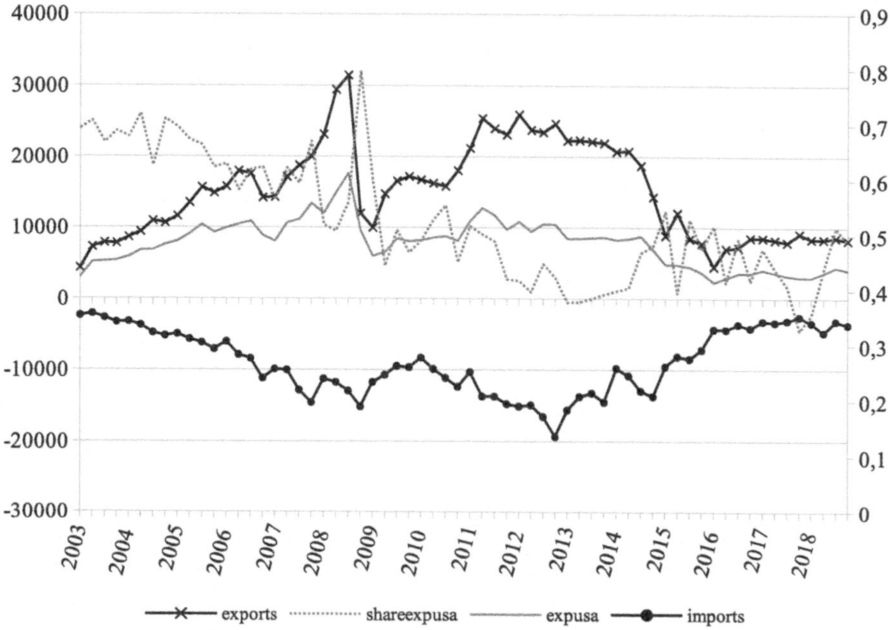

Fig. 4.7 Venezuela. Total exports and imports, exports to the United States and its share in Venezuelan total exports (right axis). US$ millions. 2003–2018. (Source: for total exports and imports, Cepal-Stat, "Sector externo, balanza de pagos trimestral"; for exports to the United States, Bureau of Economic Analysis, "U.S. International Transactions, Expanded Detail by Area and Country," Table 1.3)

The figure allows a better view of the relative importance of the changes in the American oil markets with regard to the economic crisis in Venezuela since 2013 (as the gross majority of the Venezuelan exports were constituted of crude oil): total exports and exports to the United States were closely correlated over the period. By 2004 approximately 70% of Venezuela's total exports went to the United States – almost exclusively crude oil or oil products. By mid-2008 this value exceeded 80%. American's share in Venezuela's exports declined until 2015, but then were increased again, always oscillating between 40 and 50% until 2018; the other share was progressively fulfilled by India, China, and Caribbean nations, and Europe to a lesser extent (see EIA 2019). This was a bitter irony, because as soon as the American government began more openly to confront Venezuela, this relation of economic dependence was again reinforced.

As another way of analyzing the intrinsic dependence of the economy on the oil exports for the United States, we can formulate a linear regression model with the Venezuelan non-oil GDP in chained Bolívares of 1997 as a dependent variable of the Venezuelan oil exports to the United States, here taken in US$ million.[34] For a

[34] See BCV, Table 5.2.7, "Oferta y demanda global a precios constantes de 1997 – Bolívares, Producto interno bruto no petrolero" and BEA, "U.S. International Transactions, Expanded Detail by Area and Country," Table 1.3.

dynamic relation, a lag of one quarter between exports and the GDP was introduced. A variant with the regression of first differences was also computed. The results are the following ones:

Regression 1
78 observations, 2003-2018
$GDP\ Bs._{t2} = 61326{,}3 + 2{,}14\ EXPUSA_{t1}$
$(SE\ 2492{,}08)$ $(SE\ 0{,}1936)$ $R^2 = 0{,}67$ $DW = 0{,}880$ $\hat{\sigma} = 11683{,}7$
$[t = 20{,}844]$ $[t = 12{,}454]$

Regression 1.1: first differences
78 observations, 2003-2018
$GDP\ Bs._{T2} = 68{,}19 + 0{,}03\ EXPUSA_{t1}$
$(SE\ 339{,}707)$ $(SE\ 0{,}032)$ $R^2 = 0{,}012$ $DW = 1{,}62$ $\hat{\sigma} = 3000{,}05$
$[t = 0{,}200]$ $[t = 0{,}99]$

The first regression shows the typical features of time series regressions, but even so its results are interesting because the US imports can be treated as an "exogenous" variable, with no simultaneous causality between the Venezuelan and the American economies – which provide less dubious statistical outputs. A high R^2 suggests a high correlation between the variables. However, visual inspection shows that both variables are not stationary and also a growing variance of residuals over time. The Durbin-Watson statistics suggests a moderate positive auto-correlation of errors. Regression 1 shows a very low *P-value* for β. Regression 2 gives 0.32 for this statistic (at a 5% significance level), a better Durbin-Watson (1.62) but a much lower R^2 (1%). Regression 1 only partially supports the abovementioned characterization of the economy for the 2003–2018 period, because of auto-correlation and higher variance of residuals over time.

The regression of Venezuelan total exports and the American imports from Venezuela gives better results, as the GDP is a much more complex variable. The American imports of Venezuela and Venezuela's total exports were closely linked over the period, which also shows the partial failure of Venezuela in expanding production by finding new markets for its oil. The simple linear regression model between Venezuela's total exports (*TE*) and American imports from Venezuela (*AI*), both in US$ million, and its variant computed with the first differences, are the following ones:

Regression 2
64 observations, 2003-2018
$TE = 1170{,}21 + 1{,}80\ AI$
$(SE\ 1003{,}85)$ $(SE\ 0{,}1195)$ $R^2 = 0{,}78$ $DW = 1{,}185$ $\hat{\sigma} = 3093{,}39$
$[t = 1{,}165]$ $[t = 15{,}051]$

Regression 2.1: first differences
63 observations, 2003-2018
$TE = 35{,}09 + 1{,}67\ AI$
$(SE\ 231{,}73)$ $(SE\ 0{,}142)$ $R2 = 0{,}69$ $DW = 2{,}07$ $\hat{\sigma} = 1839{,}2$

There is better result of the regression 2, shown by a high R^2, the Durbin-Watson test suggesting a lower positive auto-correlation of errors if compared to regression 1 (which takes into the account the whole economy and not only exports).[35] There is still a relatively low *P-value* for coefficient *b* for both of the regressions (significance level of 5%), which suggests that the value for coefficient 1.80 is not accurate. On the other hand, the regression of the first differences gives not only a better Durbin-Watson (2.07) but also almost the same R^2 (69%). Visual inspection for first differences in fact shows stationarity for both y and x, and stable variances for residuals, leading to more satisfactory results. It is interesting to note that the introduction of a lag between the variables (one quarter) did not improve the results, leading to a R^2 of 59% and a higher *P-Value*, both suggesting that the changes in the American markets have immediate impacts on the Venezuelan exports. Results for regression 2.1 suggest in statistical terms the final outcome of the close interrelation between oil extraction, prices, and demand between the United States and Venezuela. Almost 70% of the changes in oil exports can be explained by the trade with the United States.[36]

This is a very important empirical result. As the majority of the Venezuelan crude oil production is exported, it is not possible to claim that the performance of the Venezuelan economy determined oil extraction. Therefore, the regression can only be interpreted in one way round, which avoids an eventual simultaneous relationship between Y and X: it was not the domestic economic decline that led to falling oil exports; it was the falling exports that affected directly and indirectly the whole economy, in the form of declining revenues for investments and state expenditures, and indirectly in the form of a reduced capacity to import machines, raw material, etc. It is obvious that a reduced capacity to import can subsequently lead to difficulties in expanding the production and then the supply of oil. But the primary shock comes from the external sector of the economy; if external demand for oil was maintained somehow, the oil extraction would not be interrupted, and the de facto adopted "model" (overvalued exchange rates and ongoing import dependence, deindustrialization, diversification on the basis of service sectors) could have endured.

In this context, Venezuela could not benefit from its production quotas stablished by OPEC since 2010, losing the opportunity of profiting from curtailed or stable productions in Libya, Iran, Nigeria, Congo, Algeria, and Kuwait. In fact, according to International Energy Agency (IEA), Saudi Arabia, the United Arab Emirates, and Iraq all expanded their physical productions since 2010, OPEC decisions to stabilize supply since 2014 notwithstanding (including a reduction in 2016, according to

---

[35] Similarly, given the estimated β_2 and its standard error, the confidence interval for degrees of freedom higher than 60 at a 95% confidence level is $1.561 \leq \beta_2 \leq 2.039$.

[36] The elasticity of the Venezuelan exports in face of the American purchases declines until mid-2012 and then increases again, showing the abovementioned dependence. (For the linear relationship $Y = a + bX$, $dY/dX = b$; the elasticity can be found by calculating $b\ X/Y$ for each pair of variables; see Mills 2014.)

the official releases of meetings 169 and 170, and also PDVSA).[37] The conclusion is that the recent crisis in Venezuelan oil exports is a result of several and interrelated factors, that is, (a) declining prices in oil markets, partially explained by higher production in the United States and other non-OPEC members; (b) declining markets in the United States, due to its higher domestic production, by means of new techniques; (c) limited alternative markets coupled with growing supply in oil markets, as China's increasing imports (which grew by more than 200.000 kt between 2008 and 2016) were supplied by Russia, Saudi Arabia, Iraq, Angola, Iran, Kuwait, and Brazil; (d) these factors which were aggravated by the American sanctions. Falling foreign investments in joint ventureş operations with PDVSA can be regarded as an additional variable, particularly because of the lack of hard currency in the nation, which hampers profit remittances.

The perspectives of a booming oil sector and rising resources to finance more social policies as well as the investment in the rest of the economy, such as those described in *Plan Nación* and *Plan Patria*, did not materialize. Particularly, Venezuela's share in the American (declining) oil imports, which reached around 18% by mid-1997, dropped constantly over Chávez's and Maduro's administrations – reaching almost null values by June 2019, now under the effects of full sanctions that reached production, transport, and finance regarding not only PDVSA but all enterprises operating in Venezuela's oil sector.[38] As the Venezuelan economic growth since 2003 counted on high oil extraction as a main source of domestic expansion, the subsequent multiple crises in the oil sector can be regarded as one of the main causes of the economic decline, including the American sanctions after 2017.

4.4 A Note on the American Sanctions

It is worthwhile to make a brief mention to the more recent American sanctions, which dates back to the administration of George W. Bush.[39] There is a long list of more recent sanctions with deeper economic effects, which started during the sec-

[37] "At November 30, 2016, an agreement was reached at the headquarters of the OPEC in Vienna to establish a production of 1.97 million barrels per day of crude oil for Venezuela, resulting in a reduction of 95,000 barrels per day for the main oil sales contracts, in order to influence the stabilization of the oil market. The OPEC proposal reaffirms the commitment made by the Organization and the non-OPEC countries to freeze and reduce the oil production agreed during the meeting in Algeria in September 2016. The agreement will come into force in January 2017 and could be renewed in six months" (PDVSA 2016, p. 60).

[38] Venezuela's specific share in the American total oil imports reached 14% by mid-2001, 10% by mid-2007, an average of 8% in 2013, 5% in 2017 and 1% by the end of 2018. See "US imports from Venezuela of crude oil and petroleum products – monthly" on:

https://www.eia.gov/dnav/pet/pet_move_impcus_a2_nus_ep00_im0_mbbl_m.htm

[39] This refer to the ban on sales of parts of the American F-16 fighter aircraft to Venezuela. I thank Steve Ellner for this observation.

ond administration of Barack Obama. The "Venezuela Defense of Human Rights and Civil Society Act of 2014" aimed to "[t]o impose targeted sanctions on persons responsible for violations of human rights of antigovernment protesters in Venezuela, to strengthen civil society in Venezuela, and for other purposes." A new executive order was signed by Barack Obama in 2015. The government of the United States, as usual, behaved as if Venezuela was a colony. The White House declared:

> a national emergency with respect to the unusual and extraordinary threat to the national security and foreign policy of the United States posed by the situation in Venezuela [in 2015]. The targeted sanctions in the E.O. [executive order] implement the Venezuela Defense of Human Rights and Civil Society Act of 2014, which the President signed on December 18, 2014, and also go beyond the requirements of this legislation. (White House 2015)

This new executive order, which aimed at "Blocking Property and Suspending Entry of Certain Persons Contributing to the Situation in Venezuela," declared not to "target the people or economy of Venezuela," but included sanctions against members of the Venezuelan Supreme Court of Justice and the Venezuelan government. Officially, these two measures did not plan a direct impact on the economy, but of course any American sanction did not benefit Venezuela, and particularly its government, as regard to its relation with the world economy and especially foreign capital (both financial as well as productive). Direct investment in Venezuela dropped in 2014, as the GDP contracted by approximately 5%, and remained at relatively low levels in 2015 (see Table 4.5).

Then, during and after 2017, the American government started to put even more pressure on Venezuela. The list of sanctions was expanded. It began with a new executive order now signed by the new president Donald Trump (E.O.13808), with the prohibition of all transactions related to the issuing of new debts in 2017. According to it:

> (a) All transactions related to, provision of financing for, and other dealings in the following by a United States person or within the United States are prohibited: (i) new debt with a maturity of greater than 90 days of Petroleos de Venezuela, S.A. (PdVSA); (ii) new debt with a maturity of greater than 30 days, or new equity, of the Government of Venezuela, other than debt of PdVSA covered by subsection (a)(i) of this section; (iii) bonds issued by the Government of Venezuela prior to the effective date of this order; or (iv) dividend payments or other distributions of profits to the Government of Venezuela from any entity owned or controlled, directly or indirectly, by the Government of Venezuela. (b) The purchase, directly or indirectly, by a United States person or within the United States, of securities from the Government of Venezuela, other than securities qualifying as new debt with a maturity of less than or equal to 90 or 30 days as covered by subsections (a)(i) or (a)(ii) of this section, respectively, is prohibited. (White House 2017)

New sanctions targeting President Maduro, and then his so-called inner circle, followed over the same year (five more) and over 2018. By 2019 new sanctions against Venezuelan enterprises were introduced. These measures included sanctions against Venezuela's Central Bank, Venezuela's National Development Bank, as well as all companies enabling the shipment of Venezuela's oil to Cuba and operating in Venezuela's oil sector (particularly Russian ones). Properties of Venezuela's government and PDVSA in the United States were also blocked in the United States in 2019.

On 28 January 2019, the White House declared in its press release that "As a result of today's action, all property and interests in property of PDVSA subject to U.S. jurisdiction are blocked, and U.S. persons are generally prohibited from engaging in transactions with them." Venezuela's gold reserves in the England were also confiscated (approximately one billion dollars worth). Between 2017 and 2019, a total of more than 60 actions against Venezuela were taken by the American government.[40]

It is very difficult to estimate precisely the whole impact of these sanctions in economic terms; this estimation demands a whole new work and cannot be properly made here. It suffices to observe that, as abovementioned, those sanctions involve a broad number of variables and are partially responsible for the aggravation of the economic crisis in Venezuela over Maduro's first term. In short, they involve (a) direct and indirect losses in terms of oil exports; (b) higher interest loans for the domestic enterprises, or even their impossibility by the lack of substitutes; (c) higher costs for transport; (d) supply difficulties arising from (b) and (c), and in broader terms also (a); and (e) losses in terms of foreign investments.

As regards oil exports particularly to the United States, we saw that they were already facing a progressive drop, reaching only around US$ 5 billion by 2014; after then these values faded still more rapidly, now under the direct impacts of the measures taken from 2017 onward. The share of the Venezuelan oil exports in the total American oil imports, which once reached almost 20% by 1997, now amounted to only 1% by mid-2019.[41] If the "new normal" before the deepening of the American sanctions in 2017 was around US$ 9 billion in oil exports (according to Fig. 4.7), then Venezuela lost approximately US$ 10 billion in oil exports over 2019, when the consequences of the sanctions started to take more direct effects. This includes only the United States; a more realistic account should also consider other lost potential markets for oil exports.

The inflow of foreign investments was also affected somehow; since 2013 Venezuela has received only a fraction of the usual past amounts, which reached almost US$ 6 billion in 2012 but only US$ 769 million by 2015 and US$ 886 million by 2018 (there is no available data for 2019). If it is true that the inflow of foreign investments is always related to the growth of the domestic market – which was contracting during Maduro's first term – this is also true that foreign investments are always influenced by the kind of sanctions that the United States were imposing on Venezuela. How much was lost between 2017 and 2019, under the impacts of the sanctions? Four, five, or six billion? It is impossible to estimate exactly. In any case, we should add to these costs the losses in terms of the Venezuela's gold reserves – US$ 10 billion worth, approximately – which are now the control of the Bank of England, and also the values regarding PDVSA's properties in the United States, which were confiscated. If we finally add higher interest rates in alternative markets for international loans and higher costs for transports – or even the impossibility for

[40] The full list can be accessed on https://2009-2017.state.gov/e/eb/tfs/spi/venezuela/index.htm and https://www.state.gov/venezuela-related-sanctions/

[41] Beyond those mentioned by Figure 4.7, another source for this relations is "U.S. Imports from Venezuela of Crude Oil and Petroleum Products Monthly," available on "https://www.eia.gov/dnav/pet/pet_move_impcus_a2_nus_ep00_im0_mbbl_m.htm"

them – total costs arising from the American sanctions may easily reach US$ 30 billion for the 2017–2019 interlude, under a conservative estimation (Venezuela had an estimate amount of US$ 8 billion in foreign reserves by mid-2018). It is obvious that the deterioration of the economic conditions over Maduro's first term is also connected to these harsh conditions imposed by the United States and its main ally, the United Kingdom.

4.5 Fiscal and Monetary Policies and Inflation

In realistic terms, fiscal deficits should be considered the norm, and not the exception in underdeveloped economies. Far from being a sign of always bad administrations, fiscal results depend on broader economic conditions which in general *cannot* be determined by the governments, always tending to instability in conditions of ongoing external dependence on primary goods and endemic tax evasion. The term "developing" is a misnomer for most of the these regions, as their economic structures still rely heavily on the export of primary resources, their states being incapable of increasing taxes for those agents who can pay (the so-called soft state once defined by Myrdal [1972]). Even when compromised leaders and administrations recognize these limits and act accordingly, it is very difficult to implement qualitative changes, because of the huge domestic and foreign political opposition. Structural tax evasion and difficulties in raising taxes for those who can pay in these extroverted and internationalized economies are never mentioned in orthodox or conventional approaches; the government often seems to be the main problem and is always associated with corruption and mismanagement.[42] Particularly, the nationalization of PDVSA, in the Venezuelan case, evidently contributed to enhance the state budget in face of the endemic tax evasion and manipulation of prices, which prevail in Latin America and which are never mentioned by conservative studies.[43] But as the economic activity remained linked to the oil exports, fiscal conditions could not be improved in face of the worsened external conditions, particularly after 2013.

Table 4.7 shows fiscal results for the 1990–2014 period.[44]

Overall and primary fiscal deficits were endemic in Venezuela between 1990 and 2004. The government rose its revenues in terms of the GDP over the whole period

[42] Regarding those difficulties, Agénor and Montiel observed in realistic terms: "In most developing economies, the tax base is inadequate, the share of small-income earners is disproportionately large, and evasion is endemic, preventing the imposition of a high tax burden on the population. […] In most developing nations, high-income earners have considerable political power, making it difficult for the government to enforce tax laws" (Agénor and Montiel 2018, p. 93).

[43] For conventional approaches to fiscal policies in Venezuela which ignore these difficulties and tend to criticize only the economic policies of the government and not tax evasion, see, for example, Urdaneta et al. 2018 and Restuccia 2019.

[44] According to Gómez-Sabaíni and Morán, Venezuela's national tributary system lost approximately US$ 1.1 billion between 2005 and 2007, by means of manipulated prices of the American companies; for a broader discussion of this mechanisms see also Piketty 2014.

Table 4.7 Venezuela. Government operations (economic classification), as a percentage of GDP. 1990–2014

Years	Total revenues and grants	Total expenditure and lending minus repayments	Wages and salaries	Interest payments	Subsidies and other current transfers	Capital expenditure	Capital transfers	Overall primary balance	Overall fiscal balance
1990	23.3	25.8	4.6	3.4	7.8	2.8	1.9	1	−2.4
1991	23.5	24.5	4.4	3.4	7.4	2.9	2.3	2.4	−1
1992	17.8	21.8	5	3.4	6.8	3	2	−0.6	−4
1993	17	20	4.3	3.4	6.4	2.9	1.9	0.4	−3
1994	17.6	25.2	4.4	4.2	5.6	2.4	1.7	−3.3	−7.6
1995	16.2	20.6	3.6	4.6	6	2.9	2.3	0.1	−4.4
1996	19.9	19.2	2.6	3.9	7.7	2.2	1.8	4.5	0.6
1997	23.8	21.9	3.9	2.5	10.2	3.1	2.7	4.4	2
1998	17.4	21.4	3.8	2.6	8.9	4	3.5	−1.4	−4
1999	18	19.8	3.4	2.8	9.1	3	2.7	1	−1.7
2000	20.2	21.8	3.7	2.5	10.1	3.3	3	0.9	−1.7
2001	20.8	25.1	4.4	2.9	10.6	4.4	3.8	−1.5	−4.4
2002	22.2	26.1	4.2	4.6	8.7	5.1	3.6	0.6	−4
2003	23.4	27.8	4.3	4.7	10.1	5.5	3.8	0.3	−4.4
2004	24	25.9	3.9	3.7	10.6	5	4.6	1.8	−1.9
2005	27.5	25.9	3.5	2.9	11.3	5.8	5.4	4.6	1.6
2006	29.7	29.8	3.8	2.1	13.7	6.7	6.4	2	0
2007	28.6	25.6	3.9	1.5	12.8	5.8	5.6	4.5	3
2008	24.5	25.7	4.1	1.3	12.8	5.7	5.6	0.1	−1.2
2009	21.4	26.5	4.9	1.3	12.9	5.4	5.3	−3.7	−5
2010	19.3	22.9	5	1.5	12	2.9	2.8	−2.1	−3.6
2011	22.5	27.5	5.2	2.1	12.5	6.5	2.9	−1.8	−4
2012	23.5	28.4	5.8	2.7	14	4.8	4.6	−2.2	−4.9
2013	26.8	30.5	5.8	3.1	14.7	5.5	5.3	1.1	−2
2014	33	35.9	6.9	3	18.7	6.1	5.7	1.1	−1.9

Source: Cepal-Stat

(from 17% to 33%), a remarkable fact in face of the abovementioned difficulties involving the tax system. By means of the boom in its oil exports, primary surpluses were achieved between 2004 and 2008; overall positive results were achieved only between 2005 and 2008. As we saw, the 2008 crisis led to lower exports, and these were reflected in new fiscal deficits (primary and overall as well). Fiscal conditions were improved temporarily between 2010 and 2013, new primary positive results being attained. Then conditions worsened again, with two global deficits of 2% of the GDP in 2013–2014, despite having being followed by two primary surpluses of 1.1%. The state external debt dropped from 13% to 9.8% between 2010 and 2016, but government's internal debt grew from 14% to 21% over the same period, according to the Cepal-Stat. Interest payments were lowered during Chávez's administrations and kept stable until 2010, but more than doubled since then, giving the higher state debt arising from growing budgetary deficits. Wages in the public sector showed a stable path until 2008, amounting to 3.8% of the total current expenditures in 1998 and only 3.9% in 2007.

As a means to counter the impacts of the 2008 crisis, there was an increase in state employment, wages reaching 5.2% of the current expenditures in 2011 and 6.9% in 2016.[45] Given the interventionist policies above described, subsidies and current transfers showed the higher growth rates, amounting to 8% in 1998, 11% in 2005, 14% in 2012, and reaching 18% in 2016 – one more sign of the increasing role of the state in the economic activity. Apparently, there were large sums of the state's budget to finance domestic firms. Particularly with regard to Chávez's administrations, subsidies grew from 8.9% to 14%. As the available data is not well detailed, it is not possible to evaluate the specific destinies of these subsidies and transfers in this aggregate study.

At this moment we reach the inflation question, which showed clear "structural," multidimensional features, such as already discussed by structuralist authors. In first place (1), inflationary pressures are a permanent condition for many "developing" nations who maintain constant net trade results. Given that the Central Bank in general has the control over the hard currency (such as in Venezuela), it is obliged to print and deliver paper money to PDVSA and all exporters; in conditions of trade surpluses (such as those between 2003 and 2017, except for few years), a relevant share of these monetary resources enter the domestic markets but do not find the material goods from which it arose (particularly in the form of wages and profits), even when the monetary authorities try to absorb part of those resources by means

[45] Apparently, there is no available data regarding fiscal conditions for the 2017–2018 period (from INE, ECLAC or the Central Bank well). Data furnished by the Central Bank of Venezuela covers the 2015–2017 interlude, but only from the point of view of the national accounts, which covers only the state's final consumption expenditures. According to them, state's consumption expenditures reached 10% of the GDP in 2015 and 9% in 2016 and 2017, which suggests that the budget conditions did not run out of control over the crisis (see CBV, "Cuentas consolidadas de la nación, base 1997, en Bolívares"). However, while nominal fiscal conditions remained more or less under control, government's expenditures were covered by higher monetary emissions, this leading to an additional source of inflation particularly since 2017 (see discussion below).

of public debt.[46] Along with a heterodox conduction of monetary policies (permanent low interest rates), this process fosters inflation in structural terms (for a discussion of Venezuela's Central Bank policies since 2005, see Campbell and Cömert 2009). But this is only one aspect of the inflation problem.

A second source of high inflation (2) was related to the monetary and fiscal policies. The interrelated and complex short-run necessities, and not economic theories, drove the economic decisions of the government since 2013. Maduro's administration implemented a strong expansion of the monetary basis as a tool of last resource for preventing a still higher economic contraction, particularly since 2016. As we saw, fiscal deficits increased as a natural consequence of the downturn in exports, the rate of exchange being put under a higher control because of the drop in foreign reserves. But the larger share of the state expenditures was implemented outside the standard channels of the official accounts, by means of the Central Bank monetary emission. That is, the administration implemented a deliberate expansion of the monetary base, the direct funding of state enterprises by the Central Bank being made so as to maintain at least some degree of economic activity. The administration mixed a "soft monetary budget" for wages and investments expenditures with low real interest rates for the private sector of the economy (see also ECLAC 2018, p. 02). This instrument, obviously, was desperately implemented so as to prevent a still higher domestic downturn in face of the drop in exports (and then American sanctions), which amounted to 76% between 2013 and 2017 – a shocking performance. These unconventional economic policies thus arose as a natural consequence in order to prevent a still higher rise in unemployment. [47]

The costs of this chaotic state of affairs involved, of course, the loss of control of prices and the progressive lack of precise economic meaning for interest rates, helping to drive saving rates to minimum levels. As domestic credit to private sector soared (see ECLAC 2018, p. 7), this lack of economic meaning for interest rates, coupled with the demonetization caused by high inflation (282,972% by May 2019), could only translate itself into some physical investment (and not only short-run consumption and/or purchase of fixed assets) under the conditions of forced state

[46] In other terms: production is made; wages and profits are generated; exports leave the nation; wages and profits enter into the market, but they do not find the correspond amount of goods from which they were generated (there is more demand than supply). Under the conditions of an underdeveloped domestic supply of goods, the alternatives to reduce inflation involve (1) raising imports, which could not be made after the crisis in the balance of payments in Venezuela; (2) absorbing a share of this domestic money resources by the public debt, which cannot be completely made because workers cannot save their wages and even profits cannot be completely absorbed by public debt (as capitalists also consume).

[47] This type of economic policies since 2014 helps to explain why the official rate of unemployment seemed so low until 2017. Evidently, this was partially explained by the growing role of the state in the economy, which fostered employment rates in state enterprises. This brought a positive consequence in terms of a lower unemployment rate; but, conversely, it also meant a lower product per head in face of the falling aggregate demand. In any case, the official rate of unemployment seems to be unrealistic in light of the dimension of the economic decline. As regards these and other reasons for the apparent low rate of unemployment in Venezuela, see Perazzi et al. 2017.

expenditures, particularly in state enterprises, a goal clearly pursued by the administration under those improvised conditions. It should be observed, however, that the growth in consumer prices exceed the growth in the monetary basis in all but 2 years (2014 and 2017), which suggests that high inflation had, in fact, more roots than monetary policy itself.

In Venezuela, the inflationary process was also fed by (3) intense speculation in real and financial markets (since 2010, according to former Minister Salas), planned disinvestments and so lower supply, in line with the general trends of finance capital for non-aligned nations. The government repeatedly reported disobedience of price controls and smuggling of goods and increasing speculation against the *Bolívar* in parallel markets (the National Institute for Statistics, however, currently does not publish official data regarding these events on its website). Here, one cannot but to mention Curcio's work on the economic warfare in Venezuela, which studied with detail how the planned shortages, induced inflation, supply boycotts, and covert trade embargoes by the private sector damaged the economy over the 2000s (see Curcio 2016). Despite the increase in M1, there was a constant lack of paper money, given high inflation and, according to the government, the traffic of money outside Venezuela by gangs and criminals. The US sanctions then added on these variables, increasing costs for transport arising as one of the consequences.

The role of exchange rates should also be stressed (4): imports were stabilized by around US$ 19 billion between 2017 and 2018, but the exchange rates were devaluated by 3.39 times from 2016 to 2015 and four times between 2017 and 2016, with natural impacts in the costs of the supply of goods. That is, the drop in foreign reserves and the subsequent devaluations of the domestic currency led to higher costs for imports and also fostered exchange rate speculation, the drop in foreign reserves being taken as an additional source of inflationary pressures, despite the apparent stability in the physical supply from imports over the period. Curcio observed that as "there is no correspondence between the behaviour of the shortage rate and the total level of imports" over the period, "the main recommendation that emerges from [the] analysis [being] the urgent need to establish greater controls on the delivery of foreign exchange to the private sector and to revise the criteria for the allocation of dollars, especially when we are faced with a drop in oil prices and, therefore, a decline in national income" (Curcio 2016, p. 37–45). In this context, "the economy was caught in a feedback loop in which the rising black market exchange rate fed inflation, and increasing inflation pushed more buyers into the black market for dollars" (Weisbrot 2015, p. 215).

As regards this complex inflation issue, Vera (2017, p. 21) proposed the adoption of a semi-dollarization in Venezuela such as the implemented in Brazil and Argentina over the 1990s. The author, apparently departing from a Post-Keynesian approach, did not mention any of the abovementioned "extra-market" mechanisms of economic terrorism and speculation which were being applied by the opposition to press Maduro's administration. In fact, this was a curious depiction of the local reality. Even in the short run, the stabilization of the macroeconomic environment as well as the economic policies would not be achieved without an increase in foreign reserves. But the only way to accomplish this in the short run was to overthrow the

Table 4.8 Venezuela. Monetary indicators. 2012–2018

	Consumer prices (%)	Monetary base (%)	M1 (%)	M2 (%)	International reserves (US$ billion)	Nominal interest rates (%). Six major banks (average) – December
2012	20.1	40.8	62	57.5	29	12
2013	56.2	61.1	66	65.4	21	15.7
2014	68.5	86.5	69.5	69.1	22	19.3
2015	180.9	95.2	85.1	84.9	16	20.9
2016	274.4	144.2	116.6	116.4	10	22.3
2017	862.6	873.1	551.7	544.9	9.6	21.8
2018	130.060	38.944	53.256	5.222	8.8	21.7

Source: ECLAC 2019 and Cepal-Stat for interest rates ("Tasa de interés activa nominal – porcentage actual," also defined as "Tasa de operaciones activas, promedio de los seis principales bancos comerciales")

ruling administration and returning to the status quo which prevailed before 1999. So, the proposal of a semi-dollarization in fact meant privatizations, more internationalization, labor precarization, then the return of the IMF, etc.

Instead of conventional prescriptions, in reality a basic goal for the Venezuelan economic policy from a developmentalist perspective – socialist or not – involved the tasks of (1) preserving the social and labor advancements and the national sovereignty over the domestic natural resources achieved after 1998 coupled with (2) a viable import-substitution policy in the long run, under the ongoing scenario of low oil exports and the American embargo, together with (3) a much more resolute fight against the methods of the private sector which "is losing patience with 'coexistence' and has been waging an economic war to destabilize the Bolivarian government" (Yaffe 2015, p. 30). It could be added that, in this context, (4) a still broader agricultural policy and land distribution should be deepened, which could give the potential benefits of (i) a higher food sovereignty and less dependence on traders; (ii) reversion of the high urbanization rates; and (iii) the increase of an economic surplus decoupled from foreign markets -such as discussed by the economic plans of the government since 1998.

4.6 An Interpretation

Chávez's decision to renationalize the oil industry was certainly a crucial one in order to regain the control of the main source of *economic surplus* in the nation. The decision to put those reserves under official control is right from the point of view of Venezuela's sovereignty and control of its main natural wealth – despite all economic and political costs involved in the process, such as the strike in PDVSA between 2002 and 2003. Chávez and his political movement also rejuvenated Venezuela in many positive aspects. New social, economic, and labor rights were created. Private property was not taken as a simple dogma, the government being decided to nationalize and distribute land (with compensations) in the name of social justice and equality. At least until Maduro's first administration, elections were made and their results accepted.

They officially recognized the need for an economic diversification and the stimulation of the productive sectors, including agriculture, on a developmentalist level. After 2003 the government started to profess socialism, which should be a particular new type of socialism such as envisaged by Chávez. It included the existence of a domestic private sector, individual liberties, as well as a partial nationalization of the economy through the incentives to local self-managed firms. But the government policies were not entirely consistent regarding their own account of the Venezuelan economy and their self-declared socialist ambitions. Except for the 2003–2008 interlude, investment rates showed a poor performance. The exchange rate regime did not contribute to local production, and consumption rates were kept on high levels; the Gini coefficient showed an improvement since 2001, but remained high if compared to the most developed nations.[48] This meant that the efforts the administration partially succeeded in its efforts for wealth distribution; moreover, they remained limited, a share of the domestic consumption being unproductively spent by the rich. There was no real comprehensive or indicative national plan with physical targets, nor an expansionary macroeconomic policy centered on a competitive exchange rate regime coupled with growing investment rates.

After 2003, this model was sustained by means of a favorable boom in oil exports and its multiple impacts on the economy, in parallel with low rates of investment (gross capital formation). In this context the high trade surpluses arising from the oil boom over the 2000s were partially wasted by a high rate of growing and subsidized imports; another share of imports was used to buy capital goods which were applied to boost the domestic sector of the economy, but mainly services and infrastructure. The government sincerely supported agriculture by several institutional and political means, but domestic production had to compete with imports; there were also no restrictions to labor mobility. Agricultural production showed a severe decline over Maduro's first administration.

It is true that the social necessities of the poor population by the end of the 1990s were very urgent, given the recent past of growing poverty, and that the government was aware of that. It is also true that service sectors, supported by the government, were important from many different aspects regarding the well-being of the poor population and new economies of scale. But despite many discretionary policies, these measures led to the rejection of a real industrial policy. Accordingly, it implemented an overvalued rate of exchange so as to subsidy consumption; this also

[48] The Gini coefficient such as informed by Cepal-Stat was 420 in 2001, 379 in 2008, 388 in 2013, and 378 by 2014 (last available data); see Cepal-Stat, "Venezula, Gini Coefficient." Venezuela performed better than the Latin American average in 2014 (471). This is an import achievement, but inequality remained high when compared to the most developed nations. For example, the Inequality-adjusted Human Development Index for Venezuela reached 0.600 for Venezuela, 0.882 for Japan, and 0.889 for Norway (see United Nations Development Program, Human Development Reports, on http://hdr.undp.org/en/content/income-gini-coefficient).

meant that the government did not press the overall rate of consumption with a forced accumulation of capital. Accordingly, there was a poor performance of the rate of investment; this liberated resources for consumption in the short run, but over time this policy led to stagnated rates of gross capital formation in the overall economy. Non-productive services sectors were expanded in relative terms, and Venezuela imported three times more in per capita terms than Brazil, Argentina, Bolivia, and Ecuador until 2009.

In short, the conditions to turn Venezuela into an industrialized though underdeveloped nation fitted with a stronger agricultural sector were not achieved. The government professed socialism, but it was a soft type of socialism in comparative terms, including a large dominant role for the private sectors and land expropriations by means of negotiation and compensations. There was no forced and extensive accumulation of productive capital. Despite the official goals such as established by the government "socialist plans," the majority of the microeconomic decisions of the private economic sectors were accepted, a high share of the national savings being more or less freely wasted in the form of consumption or capital exports, in direct contrast with more rigid models of socialist or indicative planning, such as the old Soviet model or the current Chinese one, with its high savings rate, devaluated exchange rates, and restrictions to labor mobility. There was no forced mobilization of the population regarding, say their reallocation so as to guarantee an increase in the agricultural production (like the Chinese policy). There was land distribution indeed, but this did not lead necessarily to a higher supply, as food imports remained high given an ongoing over-appreciation of the domestic currency, dropping demand, low financing, and general lack of disposition toward farming.

The crisis in oil markets after 2008 represented a first shock on the functioning of the adopted economic model, which could have persisted for additional years had oil prices and exports to the United States been maintained. It should be stressed that the changes in oil markets after 2008 were very intense, contradicting the government's original previsions. The behavior of the oil prices was very unstable during the 2000s; first there was a boom that led to an overestimation of the prices for the long term, then came a huge drop, leading to a massive shock in the economy, which still largely depended on oil exports, directly and indirectly. The financial crisis of 2008 led to lower prices, as the United States started to stimulate more alternative types of energy supply from its own domestic sources; the subsequent American sanctions led to additional impacts. These conditions for oil markets led to a destabilization of the adopted economic model in Venezuela.

The nationalization of the oil industry was a great step toward the control of the economy, but lost much of its potentialities when oil prices dropped and its markets contracted. The government sought to overcome the alleged limits of the Soviet model, but the achieved results were not impressing in terms of changing the economic structure, although a more egalitarian Venezuela having been achieved over those years. Had a more rigid policy of "extensive socialist accumulation" been pursued after 2003 (when Chávez made his decisive shift), the government would have been forced to nationalize not only the oil industry or selected industries but also the majority of the main national savings and physical capital. This would have also prevented hyperinflation by means of a higher control of the supply of goods. This would have meant not only limited expropriations and the creation of new state enterprises, but also a more generalized nationalization of the economy as a whole, capital exports being restricted on a much higher level so as to preserve domestic savings, fostering a higher rate of investment by means of a devaluated exchange rate regime. Strict import and consumption controls would have been stablished since the beginning, particularly because Venezuela would have been forced to search for new trade partners than the United States since the beginning. For the success of a socialist accumulation of capital, the national currency should have been devaluated and agriculture stimulated by more resolute methods. The national savings, including trade surpluses, would have been invested mainly in selected sectors of the manufacturing and productive industries with virtual better perspectives for exports in the region (South and Central America and the Caribbean), as well as those necessary to produce domestically some of the basic or intermediate goods which the nation still imported. Accordingly, services would have lagged behind for some years. In fact, modern service sectors were historically born as a result of successful processes of capital accumulation in productive sectors, and any economic policy that focus on them before achieving the setting up of a strong manufacturing sector, coupled with adequate food supply, will face many difficulties, as we saw in Venezuela.[49] On the other hand, it is also clear that had the national savings and the national investment been kept both on higher levels, the population would have been forced to withstand more years of frugality before reaping the benefits of an extensive accumulation of capital which could allow for a higher supply of goods.

These limits for an expansionary economic policies occurred by several reasons. Theoretically, the first was time. It is never easy in political and institutional terms to abandon a mere developmentalist approach and assume a socialist one under democratic conditions. Socialism is a long-term goal and requires previous efforts in terms of propaganda, political *persuasion*, organization, and planning; and historically, it required a social revolution. But Chávez began to openly profess socialism only by 2003, and until the first economic crisis of 2008, only 5 years had

[49] "The distinction between productive and unproductive labour has sometimes been identified with the distinction between supplying goods and performing services. This has entered into the system of national income accounting used in the Soviet Union. There, final services are not included as part of the flow of production. In this context, this can be defended. It certainly does not mean that services are not important or that education and armed forces are starved of funds. The purpose of the national accounting of the Soviet Union is mainly to record the overall growth of production. For the industrial sectors, this can be shown in terms of physical production output (though changes in composition and in quality are not easy to catch) but services have to be entered in the accounts merely as salaries of those who perform them. However, this distinction between activities, such as transport, which contribute to physical output, and final services, which do not, is necessarily somewhat arbitrary. […] When we are thinking of welfare, we must consider the benefits derived from economic activity and then medical and educational services may be considered more valuable than most of the commodities sold in the shops" (Robinson 1979, p. 36).

elapsed. There were few political and economic conditions to implement "socialism" immediately, particularly because Chávez did not install a "dictatorship of the proletariat." A second element was poverty. The Venezuelan people impoverished over the 1980s and 1990s; the promise of more harsh years in the name of rapid industrialization was not an easy one in political terms. Another element is political opposition; if political conflict is being channeled through parliamentary means under the rule of law, this political opposition to more decisive methods for a rapid and equally distributed economic growth will be stronger because eventual repression must be maintained under more or less strict limits.

But it is also true that Chávez himself did not believe in more radical models of economic growth, and so he deliberately adopted economic policies which have a share of responsibility regarding the economic decline. The prejudices against the historical experiences regarding socialist or indicative planning have also played a decisive role. Departing from his particular prejudices regarding the Soviet model or its related versions, Chávez himself often seemed to be unaware of the fact that a "socialist" Venezuela needed a great deal of extensive accumulation before a diversification of the economy toward services and the free proliferation of small and middle self-managed enterprises that could more or less occur subsequently, such as in the type of socialism proposed, for example, by Alec Nove's model (see Nove 1992). The official documents showed a trust in permanent high oil prices that could, presumably, avoid the difficulties related to a deeper effort in capital accumulation.

J. Wilczynski observed:

> If new Socialist countries were established in the future, would they repeat the Eastern European extensive growth pattern? This question was examined by an East German economist, G. Kohlmey. In his view no clear-cut answer is possible, as the actual course would depend on the initial situation inherited from the preceding system: '...if the revolution is victorious in a developed industrial country,' he concluded, 'it will be possible to do without some economic measures of an extensive nature. On the other hand, in less developed countries with an extremely large population and mass unemployment, the first task will consist in finding full employment for the working people. This automatically involves an extensive process of growth...' Whatever the industrial set-up may be, in any case, the period of extensive growth, if needed at all, will not last as long as it did in the Socialist countries and need not produce the harsh bureaucratic forms of the past. (Wilczynski 1972, p. 46)

According to that, it was not the fact that Chávez was wrong regarding the many problems of a socialist economy. It was the fact that Venezuela was too underdeveloped in economic terms to implement a model of market socialism that had been historically developed for economies which (1) had previously achieved a higher degree of capital accumulation (such as the USSR or the German Democratic Republic) and/or (2) whose governments had much more comprehensive political and macroeconomic tools for controlling the economy (such as China, Cuba, Vietnam, and North Korea up to now) – which presumed a social revolution. Venezuela had none of these features, and the result is that the worst features of each model were mixed: (underdeveloped) capitalism was not abolished, including all its negative consequences, but an extensive accumulation of capital on a socialist basis was also not implemented. The government did not decide to bear most of the costs involved in the application of a higher rate of extensive accumulation, such as the temporary permanence of low standards of living, lack of supply of many consumption goods, restrictions to travel abroad, etc.; at the same time, it had to cope with the limits of democracy and the political opposition of private groups. As these economic problems were not solved through a set of expansionary macroeconomic tools centered on a competitive exchange rate and a more radical nationalization of the domestic wealth, the private, the state sectors, as well as the self-managed enterprises lacked aggregate demand given a high propensity to import and the growth of unproductive sectors. In broader terms, the Venezuelan recent economic history shows some of the main gains but also the limits of adopting a democratic and market socialism in an underdeveloped nation marked by an unequal distribution of wealth and dependence on foreign markets for natural resources.

References

Agénor PR, Montiel PJ (2018) Development macroeconomics, 4th edn. Princeton University Press, Princeton

Bernstein T (2010) Chinese agrarian policies. In: Pons S, Service R (eds) A dictionary of 20th-century communism. Princeton, Princeton University Press

Campbell A, Cömert H (2009) Progressive third world central banking and the case of Venezuela. In: Saad-Filho A, Yalman G (eds) Economic transitions to neoliberalism in middle-income countries. Routledge, London

Chávez Frías H (2013) Discursos del Presidente ante la Asamblea Nacional (1999–2012) vols I-IV Caracas, Feditorial de la Assemblea Nacional William Lara

Corrales J, Penfold M (2011) Dragon in the tropics. Brookings Institution Press, Washington, DC

Curcio P (2016) The visible hand of the market. Economic warfare in Venezuela. Caracas, Ministry of Foreign Affairs of Venezuela

Dachevsky F, Kornblihtt J (2016) The reproduction and crisis of capitalism in Venezuela under Chavismo. Lat Am Perspect 44(1):78–93

Davis R (2014) The command economy. In: Pons S, Service R (eds) A dictionary of 20th-century communism. Princeton, Princeton University Press

Economic Commission for Latin America and the Caribbean (2018) Estudio Económico de América Latina y Caribe – República Bolivariana de Venezuela. ECLAC, Santiago. https://repositorio.cepal.org/bitstream/handle/11362/43964/105/EEE2018_Venezuela_es.pdf

Economic Commission for Latin America and the Caribbean (2019) Economic survey of Latin America and the Caribbean. Santiago, ECLAC

Ellman M (2014) Socialist planning. Cambridge, Cambridge University Press

Ellner S (2017) Venezuela's fragile revolution. From Chávez to Maduro Monthly Review 69(5)

Energy Information Administration (2019) Country analysis executive summary: Venezuela. EIA, Washington, DC

Enríquez L (2013) The paradoxes of Latin America's Pink Tyde: Venezuela and the project of agrarian reform. The Journal of Peasant studies, 40(4): 611:638

Erebus W, Wen T, Sit T, Lau Kin C (2020) Legacies of China's Land Revolution of 1949. In: Jha P, Yeros P, Chambati W (eds) Rethinking the social sciences with Sam Moyo. Tulica Books, New Delhi

Felicien, Schiavoni, Romero (2018) The politics of food in Venezuela. Mon Rev 70(2)

Furtado C (1977) Economic development of Latin America. Cambridge Economic Press, Cambridge
Gallegos R (2016) Crude nation. How oil riches ruined Venezuela. Potomac Books, Lincoln
Hausmann R, Rodríguez F (eds) (2014) Venezuela before Chávez, anatomy of an economic collapse. The Pennsylvania State University
International Energy Agency (2019a) Country Analysis Executive Summary: Venezuela. https://www.eia.gov/beta/international/analysis_includes/countries_long/Venezuela/venezuela_exe.pdf
International Energy Agency (2019b) Background reference: Venezuela. https://www.eia.gov/beta/international/analysis_includes/countries_long/Venezuela/venezuela_bkgd.pdf
International Monetary Fund (1993) Balance of payments manual. IMF, New York
Jaimes E, Mendoza J, Ramos Y, Pineda N (2002) Propriedad de la tierra y la seguridad alimentaria de Venezuela. Interciencia 27(12)
Kalecki M (1968) El desarrollo de la economía socialista. Fondo de Cultura Económica, Mexico City
Lavelle D (2013) A twenty-first century socialist agriculture? Land reform, food sovereignty and peasant–state dynamics in Venezuela. Int J Sociol Agric Food 21(1):133–154
Lubbock R (2019) The hidden ediffice of (food) sovereignty: rights, territory, and the struggle for agrarian reform in Venezuela. J Agrarian Change:1–22
Mills T (2014) Analyzing economic data. New York, Palgrave Macmillan
Myrdal G (1972) Asian Drama: an inquiry into the poverty of the nations. Abridged by Seth S. King. Pantheon Books, New York
Nove A (1992) The economics of feasible socialism. Harper-Collins, London
Perazzi JR et al (2017) Análisis de la duración del desempleo y el destino de los desempleados en la República Bolivariana de Venezuela. Revista de la CEPAL 22:255–273
Petróleos de Venezuela S.A. (2010) Consolidated financial statements. PDVSA, Caracas. Available on: http://www.pdvsa.com
Petróleos de Venezuela S.A. (2011) Consolidated financial statements. PDVSA, Caracas. Available on: http://www.pdvsa.com
Petróleos de Venezuela S.A. (2016). Consolidated Financial Statements. Caracas: PDVSA. Available on: http://www.pdvsa.com
Piketty T (2014) Capital in the 21st century. Harvard University Press, Cambridge, MA
Programa Venezuelano de Educación – Acción en Derechos Humanos (PROVEA) (2019). Derecho a la tierra. Informe anual. Caracas
Purcell T (2013) The political economy of social production companies in Venezuela. Lat Am Perspect 40:146–168
República Bolivariana de Venezuela (2001a) Plan Nación 2001–2007. Gazeta Oficial de la República, Caracas. Available on: http://www.mppp.gob.ve/
República Bolivariana de Venezuela (2001c) Líneas generales del plan de desarrollo económico y social de la nación 2001–2007. Ministerio del Poder Popular de Planificación, Caracas. Available on: http://www.mppp.gob.ve/wp-content/uploads/2018/05/Plan-de-la-Nación-2001-2007.pdf
República Bolivariana de Venezuela (2007) Primer Plan Socialista de la Nación – Projeto Nacional Simón Bolívar. Gazeta Oficial de la República, Caracas. Available on: http://www.psuv.org.ve/wp-content/uploads/2011/03/Proyecto-Nacional-Simón-Bol%C3%ADvar.pdf
República Bolivariana de Venezuela (2013) Ley del plan de la patria. Segundo plan socialista de desarrollo económico y social de la nación 2013–2019. Gazeta Oficial de la República, Caracas. Available on: http://www.mppp.gob.ve/wp-content/uploads/2013/09/ley_plan_patria.pdf
Restuccia D (2019) The monetary and fiscal history of Venezuela, 1960-2016, Working paper no. 2018-59. University of Chicago, Becker Friedman Institute for Economics
Robinson J (1979) Aspects of development and underdevelopment. Cambridge University Press, Cambridge

Sutherland M (2018) La ruína de Venezuela no se deve al 'socialismo' ni a la 'revolución'. Nueva Sociedad 274

Thirlwall AP (2002) The nature of economic growth. Edward Elgard, Cheltenham

United Nations (2019) International Migration Stock 2019 – Wall Chart. New York, United Nations Population Division. Available on: https://www.un.org/en/development/desa/population/migration/publications/wallchart/docs/MigrationStock2019_Wallchart.pdf

Urdaneta A, Prieto MEP, Marilú TAZ (2018) Enfoque de la política fiscal en Venezuela en período 2000-2016. Económicas CUC 39(2):95–108

Vera L (2017) In search of stabilization and recovery: macro policy and reforms in Venezuela. J Post-Keynesian Econ 40(1):9–26

Weisbrot M (2015) Failed. What the 'experts' got wrong about the global economy. Oxford University Press, Oxford

White House (2015). Fact sheet: Venezuela Executive Order. Washington D.C. Available on: https://obamawhitehouse.archives.gov/the-press-office/2015/03/09/fact-sheet-venezuela-executive-order

White House (2017) Executive Order 13808. Washington D.C. Available on https://home.treasury.gov/system/files/126/13808.pdf or https://www.whitehouse.gov/presidential-actions/presidential-executive-order-imposing-sanctions-respectsituation-venezuela/

Wilczynski J (1972) Socialist economic development and reforms. Palgrave Macmillan, London

Yaffe H (2015) Venezuela: building a socialist communal economy? Int Crit Thought 5(1):23–41

Yergin D (2011) The quest. Energy, security and the making of the modern world. Penguin Press, New York

Chapter 5
Conclusions

For many reasons, it is not an easy task to evaluate the recent economic and social history of Venezuela; the issue refers to recent events and is also highly politicized. This study aimed to carry out a sober analysis of the recent economic and social history of Venezuela, including their achievements and failures. We shall summarize our empirical findings, which be followed by some general concluding remarks.

Regarding the economic and social achievements in Venezuela since 1998, Weisbrot rightly observes that the problem with the majority of the conventional and/or propagandistic literature on Venezuelan is that it only highlights the difficulties of implementing socialist policies, not its social gains (Weisbrot 2015, p. 221). This type of approach tends to ignore, in its allegedly "neutral" and "pro-market" analysis, that Venezuela was one more neocolonial economy in Latin America and the Caribbean at the end of the last century. The majority of the Latin American nations which followed "conventional" policies over the same period did not show better rates of improvements in social conditions. In reality, the majority of them performed worst in reducing inequality and unemployment, which resulted from a higher socialization of the means of production and a broader role for the state in coordinating some sectors of the economy, despite their already mentioned limits in doing that. These achievements since 1998 should be stressed, despite their side effect costs and the errors made by the government. Despite the economic crisis, Venezuela still had one of the best Gini coefficients in the region in 2017.[1]

In broader terms, over the last years, the majority of the Latin American and Caribbean nations lost control over their main national natural resources through privatizations and internationalization, in parallel with deprived labor rights, higher external indebtedness, and ongoing repression against social mobilization under proto-fascist and now open neocolonial administrations in the area. As a consequence

[1] See Cepal-Stat, "Índice de concentración de Gini." Despite the economic crisis, Venezuela still maintained the best results among the region over 2000–2017, including Uruguay, while Brazil appears as the most unequal in 2017.

© The Editor(s) (if applicable) and The Author(s), under exclusive license to Springer Nature Switzerland AG 2020

V. E. Schincariol, *Society and Economy in Venezuela*, SpringerBriefs in Sociology, https://doi.org/10.1007/978-3-030-60083-9_5

of long-run deindustrialization or economic involution, part of the domestic capital in the region transmuted into organized crime and drug traffic, para-militarism, and proto-fascism appearing as their political facet.[2] Venezuela showed that social mobilization and political activity can improve many aspects of the social conditions and national independence without the need for economic growth. It is a truism to say that behind the ferocity with which the Venezuelans authorities are being treated underlies the American struggle for the control of oil resources and the perpetuation of a stagnated and excluding state of affairs in the area. It is clear that these external forces do not have any national or social project to change the conditions of living of the majority in Venezuela. If the Venezuelan socialist or nationalist model could succeed, it would be another bad example for the world capitalist periphery, under the permanent "domino theory" of the American State Department.[3]

Despite these real and important achievements, the performance of the Venezuelan economy since 1998 was marked by strong fluctuations and an overall macroeconomic downward trend after the second half of the 2000s. This was a complex result of different interrelated variables, which involved the erratic performance of the foreign oil markets; the type of the adopted macroeconomic policies; the behavior of the important private groups against the "Bolivarian revolution"; and the sanctions by the United States. All these variables should be considered in a historical account of the economic downturn and then the successive crises.

In the first half of the 2000s, there was an economic recovery in Venezuela, based on growing oil exports. Budget conditions were improved and the administrations of Chávez adopted an interventionist stance, implementing new social and labor rights, land reforms, nationalizations, and subsidies extracted from PDVSA and other foreign companies. A complex, multiple but largely over-valuated exchange rate regime was maintained over the period. Accordingly, the relation of imports to the GDP grew until 2009 partially because of the higher imports of intermediate goods and machines for the non-oil sectors, but also due to basic goods. The non-oil sectors of the economy grew faster than the oil-sector until 2009, denoting some positive aspects of investing a share of the oil resources into the non-oil sectors, but manufacturing and agriculture lagged in relative terms.

---

[2] Item 2.7.6.2 of the *Plan Patria 2009–2025* (República Bolivariana de Venezuela 2018, p. 176–177) contained general outlines for a future policy of disarmament, particularly in face of the high violence levels prevailing in Venezuela.

[3] One good example refers to all issues involving migration. It is true that emigration rates in Venezuela grew after 2014. Suddenly its was depicted by the Western media as a sign of a "humanitarian crisis." According to the United Nations (United Nations 2019), immigrants living in the "democratic" Colombia amounted to 109.6 thousands by 2000 and 1142.3 thousands in 2019, many of whom probably coming from Venezuela. According to the same source, there were in Venezuelan 1013.7 thousands immigrants by 2000 and 1357.7 in 2019 (i.e., Venezuela had more immigrants than Colombia). Most of these foreigners in Venezuela were Colombians which tried to escape from poverty in the rural areas and endemic paramilitary violence, particularly against social activists. But Colombia, as an American satellite, is rarely defined as having a mix of paramilitary, "narco," and so proto-fascist state.

This brief and limited process of diversification of the economy on the basis of oil exports and services sectors was firstly interrupted by the impacts of the international financial crisis of 2008–2009 on oil markets and the global economy. This led to lower investments in PDVSA, and so lower multiplier effects in the form of wages and investments paid by the oil-sector, as well as lower fiscal results, which meant lower subsidies and state expenditures. There was a short-lived recovery in external oil markets between 2010 and 2011; this recovery was also clearly associated with a brief recovery of the domestic economy. However, oil exports started to fall again after 2012, this time much more rapidly. The economy as a whole followed the trend, the oil sector still having a dominating role in terms of the GDP change. Despite all social advances implemented over the period, the alleged "socialist" orientation of the economy did not implement a reversal of the falling rates of manufacturing and agricultural production; the private sector remained dominant. At the same time, the government faced increasing opposition, which were materialized in several forms of economic opposition; the American sanctions worsened the situation. Therefore, the economic decline which was clear since 2008, and particularly after 2013, had multiple and aggravating causes. These facts forced the administrations to maintain and/or implement unconventional tools, such as (i) price and exchange rates controls and (ii) monetization of state expenditures. This last one helped to foster inflation, which, however, had many other roots. By its turn, hyperinflation penalized wages and disrupted normal economic activity, being an additional variable of the huge economic downturn during Maduro's first term.

As the Venezuelan leaders declare to pursue socialism, some broader remarks should be done on this. Venezuela has been a laboratory of an alleged new socialist project under the new conditions of a Post-Soviet world. This implied a growing role for the state in the economy, land reform, and nationalizations, but by historical or comparative standards, the so-called Bolivarian socialism was a limited one. Labor mobility was normally allowed by means of temporary labor contracts and alike. No detailed physical targets were stablished for each enterprise, but only general targets for the GDP growth, oil extraction, and social indicators, together with a general guidelines to alter the economic structure toward a collectivist course. There was not forced accumulation of capital on an "extensive" basis of forced savings, radical wealth distribution, and generalized low consumption. A large private sector remained. And as the bunk of private sector continued to exist, most of it did not cooperate with the government, despite the practical acceptance of a "Bolivarian Bourgeoisie."[4] There was also no monopoly of the political power for the ruling party (the PSUV).

It is obvious that this hybrid model had some advantages in light of the traditional problems of the Soviet socialist model – a historical reference that was always negatively taken by Chávez – but it was also full of problems not seen in the Soviet

[4] "The government's distinction between the hostile traditional bourgeoisie and a 'friendly' emerging one has remained largely unchanged under Maduro" (Ellner 2017, p. 05).

model or the current Chinese one. It is true that there was the nationalization of the main richness of the nation – oil reserves and PDVSA – together with an incentive to self-management and other new progressive social structures (*comunas*), which should be the base of the new socialist society. Many collective new economic and social structures were fostered, partially as a means to counter speculation in food markets. Higher unemployment rates were lowered by somewhat forced means (nationalizations, higher fiscal deficits, discretionary allocation of the workforce in the public sector and higher monetary basis). These policies had many side effects, but helped to lower unemployment rates and wealth inequality.

If we could point to the major reason for Venezuela's economic decline and then the crisis, it would still be the broad performance of the oil sector, which remained decisive all over the period. As the statistical analysis suggested, there was a high correlation between the American oil imports and the Venezuelan GDP growth rates over the period; the rate of investments was also linked to the imports, which depended on the oil exports. Any significative change in this relation would lead to great impacts on Venezuela. Even a more efficient exchange rate regime would not have avoided a crisis in the face of the dimension of the crises in the oil markets. And as if the saturation in world oil supply in parallel with the new energy technologies in the United States were not enough, the nation was then damaged by several sanctions applied by its main trade partner (such as Cuba after 1959). As already observed, that adopted model of de facto hybrid economy would have endured under more favorable conditions had the external sector of the economy showed a more stable path. Theoretically, in the absence of those crises, economic policies could also have been improved under more normal conditions, including the exchange rate regime and the other policies necessary to fostering manufacturing and agriculture. Unfortunately, this did not happen.

As observed, there were also limits regarding the economic policies. Since the beginning of Chávez's first administration, economic policies did not foster by more forced means a deeper rate of investments, which should have been translated into a deeper manufacturing capacity in the tradable sectors and a deeper agricultural production. The general diagnostic of the problems of the Venezuelan economy made by Chávez and his fellows was correct, from the point of view of a developmental approach. That is, Venezuela should diversify the economy and reach food sovereignty, using the surplus coming from oil exports to foster this process. But there was a conscious decision of avoiding what could have been a "socialist primitive accumulation of capital" on the terms above defined. Although bringing many positive social and economic aspects to the nation, the socialist model as thought by Chávez was incapable of changing the economy also because of the ongoing reliance on an overvalued exchange rate regime and so limited efforts to boost investment – which assumed a much more stable path for oil markets in the near future and the overall permanence of the unequal distribution of wealth in the nation, linked to its class divisions. The ongoing high propensity to import largely erased other efforts to diversify the economy toward domestic production. The government previsions regarding the oil markets were particularly not correct, this main source of economic surplus – which sustained the adopted model – being cut by several successive crises since 2008. This wrong prevision largely explained why no forced extensive accumulation of capital was adopted since the beginning; a more stable oil market was expected by the government for the next years. The trust in the domestic private groups also backfired; the perverse functioning of the private markets over the crisis, particularly during Maduro's first administration, would not have occurred under a more rigid style of socialist planning, as historically demonstrated.

The model of a hybrid economy since 2003 meant that authorities avoided a complete planning of the economy, a large private sector in the economy being maintained, including food import and distribution. This gave some resilience to the economy until the crisis, a total abolition of private markets appearing as a naïve leftist deviation. On the other hand, insufficient domestic supply of food, ongoing dependence of the "agro-import complex," and so high speculation (despite a partial agrarian reform); planned disinvestments by private agents; capital flights; and economic terrorism were all increasingly used by the private groups to damage the economy particularly during Maduro's first term, in parallel with the American actions against the nation.[5] Venezuela's then main trade partner – the United States – became its main political enemy, a true contradiction as the American oil markets still accounted for the majority of the Venezuelan oil exports. In short, the economic decline and then the deep crisis were a result of complex and interrelated causes.

An eventual return of foreign Western loans and investments in the oil sector seem to require a regression in terms of national independence over the natural resources and labor legislation which the majority of the population would not accept. The current economic perspectives of the urbanized population also seem to exclude the possibility of contracting still more the consumption rates in order to foster savings rates. Giving the state of its oil and financial markets, and deprived of the alternative of a large number of small and medium farmers to support industrial accumulation in the cities (such as in China), the economy tends to rely almost exclusively on urban services sectors, which are incapable to finance any relevant accumulation of capital in the long run. The cultural aspects of a highly and growing urbanized population also seem to exclude this partial solution for economic decline and inflation. Thus, the Venezuelan economy now reaches an impasse, and it is still not clear how this will be solved.

In this case, it was not so clear anymore that the *pros* of the "market socialism" orientation exceeded the *contras* of a more comprehensive state control of the economy and politics. In theory, a higher socialization of the means of production could have assured a higher *extensive* growth based on forced accumulation of the national savings, coupled with more stable prices given by a broader state control of production and distribution. In this respect, in light of the dimension reached by the

[5] As Felicien, Schiavoni, and Romero observed: "There are direct parallels between present-day Venezuela and Chile in the 1970s under Salvador Allende, where the U.S. strategy, in the words of Richard Nixon, was to 'make the economy scream'. The United States employed the same methods of destabilization, including a financial blockade, and supported the right-wing counterrevolution, likewise manifested in shortages, lines, and street protests, among other forms of disruption" (Felicien et al. 2018, p. 12).

economic decline and inflation rates over the last years, the stress on the alleged benefits of a hybrid economy should be at least partially reevaluated for a nation where no previous broad socialization of the means of production have been achieved, not to mention the ongoing influence of powerful hostile domestic forces which did not fully operate in the nations where socialist revolutions once took place.

References

Ellner S (2017) Venezuela's fragile revolution. From Chávez to Maduro. Mon Rev 69(5)

Felicien, Schiavoni, Romero (2018) The politics of food in Venezuela. Mon Rev 70(2)

República Bolivariana de Venezuela (2018) Plan de Patria 2025 – hacia la prosperidad económica. Gazeta Oficial de la República. Available on, Caracas. http://www.mppp.gob.ve

Weisbrot M (2015) Failed. What the 'experts' got wrong about the global economy. Oxford University Press, Oxford

Appendix

Sources and References

Sources

Statistics

Central Bank of Venezuela: http://www.bcv.gov.es
Economic Commission for Latin America and the Caribbean – Cepal-Stat: https://cepalstat-prod.cepal.org/
Gaceta Oficial de Venezuela: http://www.tsj.gob.ve/gaceta-oficial
Instituto Nacional de Estadística (INE): https://www.ine.gov.ve
International Energy Agency: https://www.iea.org
Ministerio del Poder Popular de la República Bolivariana de Venezuela: http://www.mppp.gob.ve
OPEC: https://www.opec.org
United Nations Population Division: https://www.un.org/en/development/desa/population/migration/data/estimates2/estimates19.asp
United Nations Development Program, Human Development Reports: http://hdr.undp.org/en/content/income-gini-coefficient
United States Department of State: https://www.state.gov/venezuela-related-sanctions/ and https://2009–2017.state.gov/e/eb/tfs/spi/venezuela/index.htm

Official Documents

Petróleos de Venezuela S.A. (2016). Consolidated Financial Statements. Caracas: PDVSA. Available on http://www.pdvsa.com
Petróleos de Venezuela S.A. (2011). Consolidated Financial Statements. Caracas: PDVSA. Available on http://www.pdvsa.com
Petróleos de Venezuela S.A. (2010). Consolidated Financial Statements. Caracas: PDVSA. Available on http://www.pdvsa.com

© The Editor(s) (if applicable) and The Author(s), under exclusive license to Springer Nature Switzerland AG 2020

V. E. Schincariol, *Society and Economy in Venezuela*, SpringerBriefs in Sociology, https://doi.org/10.1007/978-3-030-60083-9

República Bolivariana de Venezuela (2019). *Linea del tiempo de la revolución bolivariana*. Caracas: Gaceta Oficial de la República. Available on http://www.mppp.gob.ve

República Bolivariana de Venezuela (2018). *Plan de Patria 2025 – hacia la prosperidad económica*. Caracas: Gaceta Oficial de la República. Available on http://www.mppp.gob.ve

República Bolivariana de Venezuela (2013). *Ley del plan de la patria. Segundo plan socialista de desarrollo económico y social de la nación 2013–2019*. Caracas: Gaceta Oficial de la República. Available on http://www.mppp.gob.ve/wp-content/uploads/2013/09/ley_plan_patria.pdf

República Bolivariana de Venezuela (2012). *Ley Orgánica del Trabajo de los Trabajadores y Trabajadoras* (LOTTT). Caracas: Gaceta Oficial de la República. Available on https://oig.cepal.org/sites/default/files/2012_leyorgtrabajo_ven.pdf)

República Bolivariana de Venezuela (2010). *Ley de Tierras y Desarrollo Agrario*. Caracas: Gaceta Oficial de La República.

Available on http://extwprlegs1.fao.org/docs/pdf/ven183010.pdf

República Bolivariana de Venezuela (2007). *Primer Plan Socialista de la Nación – Projeto Nacional Simón Bolívar.* Caracas: Gaceta Oficial de la República. Available on http://www.psuv.org.ve/wp-content/uploads/2011/03/Proyecto-Nacional-Simón-Bol%C3%ADvar.pdf)

República Bolivariana de Venezuela (2006). *Ley orgánica de hidrocarburos*. Caracas: Gaceta Oficial de la República. Available on www.pdvsa.com

República Bolivariana de Venezuela (2001). *Plan Nación 2001–2007.* Caracas: Gaceta Oficial de la República. Available on http://www.mppp.gob.ve/

República Bolivariana de Venezuela (2001b). *Decreto con fuerza de ley de tierras y desarrollo agrario*. Caracas: Gaceta Oficial de la República. Available on http://extwprlegs1.fao.org/docs/pdf/ven28661original.pdf

República Bolivariana de Venezuela (2001c). *Líneas generales del plan de desarrollo económico y social de la nación 2001–2007.* Caracas: Ministerio del Poder Popular de Planificación. Available on http://www.mppp.gob.ve/wp-content/uploads/2018/05/Plan-de-la-Nación-2001-2007.pdf

República Bolivariana de Venezuela (1999). *Constitución de La República Bolivariana de Venezuela.* Caracas: Gaceta Oficial. Available on https://pdba.georgetown.edu/Constitutions/Venezuela/ven1999.html

White House. Economic Report of the President (2019). Washington, DC. Available on https://www.whitehouse.gov/wp-content/uploads/2019/03/ERP-2019.pdf

References

Adizes I (1977) Autogestión: la práctica yugoslava. Mexico City, Fondo de Cultura Económica
Agénor PR, Montiel PJ (2018) Development macroeconomics, 4th edn. Princeton University Press, Princeton
Azzellini D (2009) Venezuela's solidarity economy: collective ownership, expropriation, and workers' self-management. WorkingUSA: J Labor Soc 12:171–1971
Baran P (1957) The political economy of growth. Monthly Review Press, New York
Barbosa WN (2017) One hundred years of learning: The Russian Revolution of 1917. Agrarian South 6(2):221–236
Bartley K, O'Brian D (2003) The revolution will not be televised (documentary). Los Angeles, Vitagraph Films
Bernstein T (2010) Chinese agrarian policies. In: Pons S, Service R (eds) A dictionary of 20th-century communism. Princeton, Princeton University Press
Betancourt R (2006) Selección de escritos políticos (1929–1981). Caracas, Fundación Rómulo Betancourt
Bistoletti EL (2011) Estudio sobre los orígines del Chavismo. Editorial Académica Española, Madrid
Brading R (2013) Populism in Venezuela. Routledge, London
Brown A (2009) The rise and fall of communism. Harper-Collins, New York
Bruce I (2008) The real Venezuela. Pluto Press, Norwich
Brus W (1973) The economics and politics of socialism, collected essays. Routledge, London
Brus W (1990) Market socialism. In: Eatwell J, Milgate M, Newman P (eds) Problems of the planned economy. Macmillan, London
Brus W, Laski K (1991) From Marx to market. Oxford University Press, Oxford
Bulmer-Thomas V (2003) The economic history of Latin America since independence. Cambridge University Press, Cambridge
Campbell A, Cömert H (2009) Progressive third world central banking and the case of Venezuela. In: Saad-Filho A, Yalman G (eds) Economic transitions to neoliberalism in middle-income countries. Routledge, London
Cano W (1999) Soberania e política econômica na América Latina. São Paulo, Edunesp
Cardoso FH, Faletto E (1979) Dependency and development in Latin America. University of California Press, Berkeley
Carrol R (2013) Comandante, Hugo Chávez's Venezuela. Penguin Press, London
Chávez Frías H (2005) Selección de discursos del Presidente de la República Bolivariana de Venezuela, vols 1–8. Ediciones de la Presidencia de la República, Caracas
Chávez Frías H (2009) Introduction. In: Brown M (ed) The Bolivarian Revolution. Verso, London

© The Editor(s) (if applicable) and The Author(s), under exclusive license to Springer Nature Switzerland AG 2020

V. E. Schincariol, *Society and Economy in Venezuela*, SpringerBriefs in Sociology, https://doi.org/10.1007/978-3-030-60083-9

Chavez Frías H (2012) Golpe de Timón. I Consejo de Ministros del nuevo ciclo de la Revolución Bolivariana. Ediciones Correo del Orinoco, Caracas

Chávez Frías H (2013 [1991]) El Libro Azul. Gobierno de Venezuela, Caracas

Chávez Frías H (2013b) Discursos del Presidente ante la Asamblea Nacional (1999–2012), vols I–IV. Feditorial de la Assemblea Nacional William Lara, Caracas

Chávez Frías et al (1992) Una propuesta. ¿Y como salir de este labirinto? In: El Correo Boliviariano. Movimiento Revolucionário – 200. Available on https://dolartoday.com/este-es-el-documento-original-de-chavez-llamando-la-transicion-firmas/

Ciccarielo-Maher G (2016) Building the commune. Radical democracy in Venezuela. Verso, London

Clairmont F (2007) Cuba and Venezuela, the nemeses of imperialism. Malaysia, Citizens International

Corrales J, Penfold M (2011) Dragon in the tropics. Brookings Institution Press, Washington, DC

Curcio P (2016) The visible hand of the market. Economic warfare in Venezuela. Ministry of Foreign Affairs of Venezuela, Caracas

Dachevsky F, Kornblihtt J (2016) The reproduction and crisis of capitalism in Venezuela under Chavismo. Lat Am Perspect 44(1):78–93

Davis R (2014) The command economy. In: Pons S, Service R (eds) A dictionary of 20th-century communism. Princeton, Princeton University Press

Di John J (2009) From windfall to curse? Oil and industrialization in Venezuela, 1920 to the present. University Park, Pennsylvania University Press

Dieterich H (2005) Hugo Chávez y el socialismo del siglo XXI. Instituto Municipal de Publicaciones, Caracas

Donghi TH (1975) História da América Latina. Paz e Terra, Rio de Janeiro

Dos Santos FL (2016) A crise da esquerda brasileira em perspectiva latino-americana. Editora Elefante, São Paulo

Dos Santos FL (2018) Uma história da onda progressista Sul-Americana (1998–2016). Editora Elefante, São Paulo

Dos Santos FL (2019) Power and impotence. A history of South America under progressivism (1998–2016). Leiden, Brill

Eatwell J, Milgate M, Newman P (eds) (1990) Problems of the planned economy. Macmillan, London

Economic Commission for Latin America and the Caribbean (2016) Economic survey of Latin America and the Caribbean. ECLAC, Santiago

Economic Commission for Latin America and the Caribbean (2018) Estudio Económico de América Latina y Caribe – República Bolivariana de Venezuela. ECLAC, Santiago. https://repositorio.cepal.org/bitstream/handle/11362/43964/105/EEE2018_Venezuela_es.pdf

Economic Commission for Latin America and the Caribbean (2019) Economic survey of Latin America and the Caribbean. ECLAC, Santiago

Elizalde RM, Báez L (2004) Chávez nuestro. Casa Editora Abril, La Habana

Ellman M (2014) Socialist planning. Cambridge University Press, Cambridge

Ellman M, Kontorovich V (1992) The disintegration of the Soviet System. Routledge, London

Ellner S (2017) Venezuela's fragile revolution. From Chávez to Maduro. Mon Rev 69(5)

Energy Information Administration (2019) Country analysis executive summary: Venezuela. EIA, Washington, DC

Enriquez L (2013) The paradoxes of Latin America's Pink Tyde: Venezuela and the project of agrarian reform. J Peasant Stud 40(4):611–638

Erebus W, Wen T, Sit T, Lau Kin C (2020) Legacies of China's Land Revolution of 1949. In: Jha P, Yeros P, Chambati W (eds) Rethinking the Social Sciences with Sam Moyo. Tulica Books, New Delhi

Ewell J (1994) Venezuela since 1930. In: Bethell L (ed) The Cambridge history of Latin America vol VIII. Cambridge University Press, Cambridge

Felicien, Schiavoni, Romero (2018) The politics of food in Venezuela. Mon Rev 70(2)

Ffrench-Davis R The Latin American economies, 1950–1990. In: Bethell L (ed) The Cambridge history of Latin America, vol VI. Cambridge University Press, Cambridge
Fürst J, Pons S, Selden M (eds) (2017) The Cambridge history of communism, vol III. Cambridge University Press, Cambridge
Furtado C (1977) Economic development of Latin America. Cambridge Economic Press, Cambridge
Furtado C (1997) Obra autobiográfica Tomo III. Paz e Terra, Rio de Janeiro
Furtado C (2008) Ensaios sobre a Venezuela: subdesenvolvimento com abundância de divisas. Contraponto, Rio de Janeiro
Gallegos R (2016) Crude nation. How oil riches ruined Venezuela. Potomac Books, Lincoln
Golinger E (2006) The Chávez Code, cracking US intervention in Venezuela. Olive Branch Press, Nothampton
Gomez-Sabaíni JC, Morán D (2016) Evasión tributária en América Latina. Nuevos y antigos desafíos en la cuantificación del fenómeno en los países de la región. ECLAC/United Nations, Santiago. https://repositorio.cepal.org/bitstream/handle/11362/39902/1/S1600017_es.pdf
Gonzalez M (2014) Hugo Chávez, socialist for the twenty-first century. Pluto Press, Ewards Bros
Gott R (2005) Hugo Chávez and the Bolivarian revolution. Verso, London
Guevara A (2005) Chávez, Venezuela and the new Latin America, an interview with Hugo Chávez by Aleida Guevara. Ocean Press, New York
Gujarati D, Porter D (2009) Basic econometrics. McGraw-Hill, New York
Harnecker M (2005) Understanding the Venezuelan revolution. Hugo Chávez talks to Marta Harnecker. Monthly Review, New York
Hausmann R, Rodríguez F (eds) (2014) Venezuela before Chávez, anatomy of an economic collapse. The Pennsylvania State University
Hawkins K (2010) Venezuela's Chavismo and populism in comparative perspective. Cambridge University Press, Cambridge
Hobsbawm E (1994) The age of extremes. Penguin Books, London
Hobsbawm E (2016) Viva la Revolución, Hobsbawm on Latin America. Little Brown, London
International Energy Agency (2019a) Country analysis executive summary: Venezuela. https://www.eia.gov/beta/international/analysis_includes/countries_long/Venezuela/venezuela_exe.pdf
International Energy Agency (2019b) Background reference: Venezuela
International Monetary Fund (1993) Balance of payments manual. IMF, New York. https://www.eia.gov/beta/international/analysis_includes/countries_long/Venezuela/venezuela_bkgd.pdf
Jaguaribe H (1967) Problemas do desenvolvimento latino-americano. Civilização Brasileira, Rio de Janeiro
Jaguaribe H (1976) Crises e alternativas da América Latina. Perspectiva, São Paulo
Jaimes E, Mendoza J, Ramos Y, Pineda N Propriedad de la tierra y la seguridad alimentaria de Venezuela. Interciencia 27(12)
Jones B (2008) ¡Hugo! The Hugo Chávez story from mud hut to perpetual revolution. Steerforth Press, New Hampshire
Kalecki M (1968) El desarrollo de la economía socialista. Mexico City, Fondo de Cultura Económica
Kantorovich L (1965) The best use of economic resources. Pergamon Press, Oxford
Kornai Y (2008) From socialism to capitalism. CEU Press, Budapest
Kovalik D (2019) The plot to overthrow Venezuela. Hot Books, New York
Lander E (2019) Crisis civilizatoria, experiencias de los gobiernos progresistas y debates en la izquierda latinoamericana. Guadalajara, Calas
Lange O (1936) On the economic theory of socialism, part 1. Rev Econ Stud 4(1):53–71
Laski K, Brus W (1991) From Marx to market. Socialism in search of an economic system. Oxford University Press, Oxford
Lavelle D (2013) A twenty-first century socialist agriculture? Land reform, food sovereignty and peasant–state dynamics in Venezuela. Int J Sociol Agric Food 21(1):133–154

Lea D (2001) A political chronology of the Americas. Europa Publications, London
Love J (1994) Economic ideas and ideologies in Latin America since 1930. In: Bethell L (ed) The Cambridge history of Latin America, vol VIII. Cambridge University Press, Cambridge
Löwy M (1999) O marxismo na América Latina. Perseu Abramo, São Paulo
Lubbock R (2019) The hidden ediffice of (food) sovereignty: rights, territory, and the struggle for agrarian reform in Venezuela. J Agrarian Change:1–22
Mancilla AS (2014) El pensamiento económico de Hugo Chávez. Quito, Instituto de Altos Estudios Nacionales
Mandel E (1962) Traité d'économie marxiste, tome 2. René Juliard, Paris
Martinez C, Fox M, Farrel J (eds) (2010) Venezuela speaks! Voices from the grassroots. PM Press, Oakland
Martins CE (2007) Venezuela. In: Sader E, Jinkings I (eds) Enciclopédia Contemporânea da América Latina e do Caribe. Boitempo, São Paulo
Mazower M (1999) Dark continent. Penguin Books, London
Mills T (2014) Analyzing economic data. Palgrave Macmillan, New York
Mommer B (2001) Venezuela, política y petróleos. In: Valecillos H, Bello O (eds) La economía contemporánea de Venezuela. Central Bank of Venezuela, Caracas
Moniz Bandeira LA (2016) A desordem mundial, o espectro total da dominação. Civilização Brasileira, Rio de Janeiro
Morón G (2004) Historia contemporánea de Venezuela. Fondo de Cultura Económica, Ciudad de México
Myrdal G (1972) Asian Drama: an inquiry into the poverty of the nations. Abridged by Seth S. King. Pantheon Books, New York
Nove A (1992) The economics of feasible socialism. Harper-Collins, London
Nove A, Nuti DM (1972) Socialist economics. Penguin Books, London
Ottero GS (2014) Hugo Chávez y la ressucción de un pueblo. Instituto Cubano del Libro, La Habana
Partido Socialista de Venezuela Unificado (PSUV) (2010) El Libro Rojo. Documentos fundamentales, Caracas
Perazzi JR et al (2017) Análisis de la duración del desempleo y el destino de los desempleados en la República Bolivariana de Venezuela. Revista de la CEPAL 22:255–273
Piketty T (2014) Capital in the 21st century. Harvard University Press, Cambridge, MA
Piketty T (2019) Capital et ideologie. Les Livres du Nouveau Monde, Seuil
Pons S, Service R (2010) A dictionary of 20th-century communism. Princeton University Press, Princeton
Programa Venezuelano de Educación – Acción en Derechos Humanos (PROVEA) (2019) Derecho a la tierra. Informe anual, Caracas
Purcell T (2013) The political economy of social production companies in Venezuela. Lat Am Perspect 40:146–168
Ramonet I Hugo Chávez (2013) Mi primera vida, conversaciones con Hugo Chávez. Barcelona, Debate
Ramonet I Hugo Chávez (2016) My first life, conversations with Hugo Chávez. Verso, London
Restuccia D (2019) The monetary and fiscal history of Venezuela, 1960–2016. University of Chicago, Becker Friedman Institute for Economics, Working paper no. 2018-59
Rivero O (2001) El mito del desarrollo. Fondo de Cultura Económica, Lima
Robinson J (1979) Aspects of development and underdevelopment. Cambridge University Press, Cambridge
Robinson J, Eatwell J (1973) An introduction to modern economics. Macgraw-Hill, London
Sader E, Jinkings I (eds) Enciclopédia Contemporânea da América Latina e do Caribe. Boitempo, São Paulo
Salas Rodríguez L (2014) Escritos desde la guerra económica. Caracas, Fundación Editorial El Perro y la Rana

Schiavoni C, Camacaro W The Venezuelan effort to build a new food and agriculture system. Mon Rev 69(3)

Schurster K, Araujo R (eds) (2015) A era Chávez e a Venezuela no tempo presente. Edupe, Rio de Janeiro

Strønen IA (2017) Grassroots politics and oil culture in Venezuela, the revolutionary petro-state. Palgrave Macmillan, London

Sutherland M (2018) La ruína de Venezuela no se deve al 'socialismo' ni a la 'revolución'. Nueva Sociedad 274

Tarver HM, Frederick JC (2005) The history of Venezuela. Greenwood Press, London

Thirlwall AP (2002) The nature of economic growth. Edward Elgard, Cheltenham

Tomba L (2010) Socialist market economy. In: Pons S, Service R (eds) A dictionary of 20th-century communism. Princeton University Press, Princeton

United Nations (2019) International migration stock 2019 – wall chart. New York, United Nations Population Division. Available on: https://www.un.org/en/development/desa/population/migration/publications/wallchart/docs/MigrationStock2019_Wallchart.pdf

Urdaneta A, Prieto MEP, Marilú TAZ (2018) Enfoque de la política fiscal en Venezuela en período 2000–2016. Económicas CUC 39(2):95–108

Vasapollo L (2013) Tratado de métodos de análisis de los sistemas económicos, mundialización capitalista y crisis sistémica. Banco Central de Venezuela, Caracas

Vera L (2017) In search of stabilization and recovery: macro policy and reforms in Venezuela. J Post-Keynesian Econ 40(1):9–26

Weisbrot M (2015) Failed. What the 'experts' got wrong about the global economy. Oxford University Press, Oxford

Wilczynski J (1972) Socialist economic development and reforms. Palgrave Macmillan, London

Wilczynski J (1981) An encyclopedic dictionary of Marxism, socialism and communism. Macmillan Reference Books, London

Wilpert G (2007) Changing Venezuela by taking power. Verso, London

Yaffe H (2015) Venezuela: building a socialist communal economy? Int Crit Thought 5(1):23–41

Yergin D (2011) The quest. Energy, security and the making of the modern world. Penguin Press, New York

Zahonero LA (2017) Chavismo. In: Moreiras A, Villacañas JL (eds) Conceptos fundamentales del pensamiento latinoamericano actual. Biblioteca Nueva, Madrid

Index

© The Editor(s) (if applicable) and The Author(s), under exclusive license to Springer Nature Switzerland AG 2020

V. E. Schincariol, *Society and Economy in Venezuela*, SpringerBriefs in Sociology, https://doi.org/10.1007/978-3-030-60083-9

The manufacturer's authorised representative in the EU is Springer Nature Customer Service Centre GmbH, Europaplatz 3, 69115 Heidelberg, Germany. If you have any concerns regarding our products, please contact ProductSafety@springernature.com

Printed and bound by CPI Group (UK) Ltd, Croydon, CR0 4YY

30/09/2026

02225664-0014